SO-ATM-241

Communism

From Marx's *Manifesto* to 20th-Century Reality

James D. Forman

Published by
Dell Publishing Co., Inc.
1 Dag Hammarskjold Plaza
New York, New York 10017

Copyright © 1972 by James D. Forman
Reprinted with revisions, 1974
All rights reserved. For information address
Franklin Watts, Inc., New York, New York 10019.
Laurel-Leaf Library ® TM 766734, Dell Publishing Co., Inc.

ISBN: 0-440-94611-5

RL: 8.3

Reprinted by arrangement with Franklin Watts, Inc.
Printed in the United States of America
First Laurel-Leaf printing—October 1976
Second Laurel-Leaf printing—April 1980

Dell books are available at discounts in quantity lots for
sales promotion, industrial, or fund-raising use. Special
books can also be created by Dell for the specific needs
of any business.

For details contact the Special Marketing Division, Dell
Publishing Co., Inc., 1 Dag Hammarskjold Plaza, New
York, N.Y. 10017

This one is for William Calder III.
He knows why.

Contents

Communism Defined

In 1848, Karl Marx and Friedrich Engels began their *Communist Manifesto* with prophetic confidence: "A spectre is haunting Europe, the spectre of communism." Little more than a century later, one third of the world's population lives under governments professing communism. Yet of this multitude less than fifty million are members of the Communist party, and not one of these could realistically say that the societies that they have achieved through massive toil, dedication, courage, treachery, and blood represent true communism.

Marx took the name for his ideal society from the French communes, feudal villages that held land and produce in common, but he was not satisfied with villages. His dream was of newly industrialized Europe shaped into a Communist world. As he saw it, other systems would give way or, if they fought back, be destroyed.

With the birth of the industrial age in the early nineteenth century, privately owned factories employed larger and larger work forces. The owners of these factories made vast profits, which they plowed back into building more factories. The worker was becoming a mere cipher in an anonymous crowd, alienated from the product of his toil.

Labor was hard, often dangerous, and poorly rewarded. This was the economic system of capitalism in its formative years, and Marx saw it leading only to increased enrichment of the owners of great businesses and the eventual enslavement of the working class.

Marx exhorted the workers to revolt. He urged them in his writings to seize the factories from the capitalists, not in order to become capitalists themselves, but in order to place the means of production in the hands of the community for the benefit of all citizens. This intermediate society controlling the means of production is called the dictatorship of the proletariat. It is what Soviet Russia and other so-called Communist nations have actually achieved, but it is not communism. True communism comes only with the further step of the state giving ownership back to the people, who continue to live together in abundance without supervision from a ruling class.

Pure communism does not exist in actual fact and probably never will. It is the carrot always held before the sweating mule. It is Eden come again, not alone for the delight of Adam and Eve, but for every man. Despite endless oration and voluminous writing on the subject of communism, almost all of this verbiage has been devoted to the struggle to achieve socialism. Today, for the commissar who drives and the worker and peasant who pull the load, communism still remains the goal, the end of struggle.

Though Marx and all his disciples have insisted and continue to insist that socialism is only a way station on the road to communism, they have not dared to describe this final paradise on earth except in the sketchiest terms. With the final achievement of communism, greed and competition will presumably cease. Each person will contribute according to his ability and receive according to his need. There will be no cause for crime or vice of any kind, no race or class rivalry, no grounds for war, and no reason for government. Perfection indeed, but unhappily not yet of this world. In fact, it is no measurably nearer than when Marx first conceived it.

Though other nations drawn to socialism do not see it necessarily as an end to socioeconomic evolution, they do not postulate communism as a necessary next or final stage. Britain, where capitalism began, now operates largely under a socialist system. Slow evolution by way of free election has been responsible for this continuing change. Communists reject such democratic socialism, maintaining that a system with more than one political party inevitably permits the confrontation between capitalists and workers. They feel that a small party of convinced Communists must steer a socialist society in the best interest of all the people.

For the purposes of this study to discover the situation of communism in the world today, we will consider three basic elements as characteristic of a Communist state. First, there is state ownership of the principal means of production. Second, there is totalitarianism, with government control firmly in the hands of a minority—in this case, dedicated Communists. Finally, there exists the messianic purpose: the eventual establishment of the ideal world community called communism.

Pre-Communism

Since Adam and Eve were cast out of Eden, man has dreamed of a return to earthly bliss. When he despaired in this hope, religion offered him paradise after death, a qualified and often dubious substitute. In ancient Greece, Plato hypothesized a perfect state in his *Republic*, which was to be ruled by philosophers and protected by a class of dedicated guardians. Wealth and education were to be communal, but Plato did not have the industrial age to deal with, nor did he eliminate from his ideal state class distinctions or the institution of slavery.

Ancient Rome was generally unconcerned with its social organization, but one strongly communistic effort came from a slave, Spartacus, who led a rebellion of slaves against the Roman legions and very nearly prevailed. During the brief years of this insurrection, the embattled society of slaves existed in a communist type of community, and Spartacus remains a hero in Soviet literature.

England contributed its pre-Marxists. In the sixteenth century, Sir Thomas More wrote of an imaginary island country where all property and produce were socialized. He called it "Utopia," from the Greek word for "nowhere," and Marx in his time would find fault with it because More offered no scientific steps for its realization. John Locke, the classical economist, saw every man as possessing property in his own person: that is, the labor of his body. But Locke was thinking of farmers and artisans and not of the factory worker to come. Substituting action for words were the Levellers, a group formed of rebel soldiers during the English Civil War. Their goal was to level estates for the benefit of peasants and artisans, but they were before their time and their movement never received wide support.

A most influential social thinker of the eighteenth century was the Frenchman Jean Jacques Rousseau, who published *The Social Contract* in 1762. This work advanced the idea that men could attain harmony by making a social contract among themselves, remaining their own sovereigns after the contract was made. Rousseau's thoughts were acted upon by the instigators of the American Revolution and were even more responsible for the French Revolution that followed. Though its goal was not socialist, the French Revolution remains a landmark in the march of socialism, for it destroyed a monarch and became an impetus and a warning for future revolutionaries. It gave full rein to the mindless power of a bourgeoisie backed by hungry peasants, which in the end led to chaos, leaving a leadership gap in France that was filled by Napoleon. This revolutionary bloodletting caused alarm as far away as Catherine the Great's Russia.

Early Communism

From popular rebellions and the Napoleonic Wars that followed, western Europe, led by Britain, stumbled into the Industrial Revolution. There had been no preparation. It was a new game without rules, and if one was wealthy enough and ruthless enough, one became a capitalist. One hired factory labor to work the new machinery, paid as little wage as possible, and had no responsibility for injuries on the job. There were no such things as social security, sickness pay, or labor unions. The workers lived in ignorance and squalor and had no prospects beyond long hours of toil and an early death. It wasn't long before the voice of reform was raised by such writers as Charles Dickens, and it was with the attitude of a charitable and repentant Scrooge that Britain moved toward labor reforms and socialism.

Karl Marx   The process of reform was slow, and its voice was not loud enough for Karl Marx. Born in Trier in the Rhineland, Germany, the son of a lawyer of Jewish descent, Marx studied at the universities of Bonn and Berlin, becoming in the process first a devout follower of the German idealist Georg Wilhelm Hegel and then a radical social philosopher obsessed with a desire to improve the lot of the worker. He was expelled from one country after another for expressing his views and encouraging unrest, and eventually he joined the Communist League. Soon after, the league moved to London, England, where it changed its name to the Federation of the Just. In 1847, working in Brussels with the help of Friedrich Engels, a German Socialist, Marx wrote the *Communist Manifesto*. It was published the next year, and Marx was subsequently expelled from Belgium and followed the league to London.

The *Manifesto*, a brief pamphlet, contained a summary of Marx's whole social philosophy and sounded to an unheeding world the first trumpet of world revolution to come. Nineteen years later the first volume of a weightier three-volume set would appear, entitled *Das Kapital*, which, together with the *Manifesto*, would become the Communist scripture, the most influential writing of the nineteenth century. In essence, the goal these works announced was the emancipation of the laboring man from the economic tyranny of the capitalist few. In building their theoretical explanation of the way in which history and economics function—a theory they called dialectical materialism—Marx and Engels relied on the following major principles.

Dialectical Materialism The first principle in the scheme is historical determinism, meaning that history is governed by natural laws, which the mind can ascertain and which make it possible for man to interpret the future. Second come the laws of history themselves. In this respect Marx was much influenced by Hegel, who had seen the historical process as one of opposing forces whose struggle leads to change. Hegel called this process of historical change the dialectic. Marx urged revolution wherever social structures had reached a stage where change was inevitable.

Coupled with this third notion of violent historical struggle is the fourth point, Marx's economic interpre-

tation of history. Beneath all historical change, the
ideas, the institutions, the laws, even the religious prac-
tices, Marx regarded the evolving economy as fundamental. This concept was related to classical materialism, which defined man and nature as fixed products of
natural law. But Marx went further to animate this
stagnant concept and reach his final principle of dialectical materialism, the idea of the economic struggle that
makes it possible for man to master the world he lives
in and improve it. The whole process of history, for
Marx, was a continuing struggle between hostile economic interests. The conflict, as he saw it developing
inevitably in the nineteenth century, matched the increasingly wealthy capitalist class against the increasingly numerous and deprived workers. The Marxist system
he developed offered both a means of understanding
society—and a program for changing it.

All this Marx conceived with the rigid certainty of
Holy Writ. As capitalism perfected itself technically,
the supply of available goods produced would gradually outrun customer demand. As a result, Marx
predicted, profits would decline, and the grasping capitalist would make up his losses at the expense of the
worker who was obliged to sell himself, not for the
value of what he could produce, but for the value of
his labor as established by the capitalist. Clearly the
latter's profits were in conflict with the former's wages,
and sooner or later a class struggle had to result.

As Marx could not imagine bourgeois capitalists
giving up their privileges voluntarily, he advocated violent revolution. The first practical step would be the
formation of political parties and trade unions of workers. Once organized, the workers would revolt. By sheer
force of numbers, they would take over and impose
their will under a dictatorship of workers, otherwise
known as the proletariat. With the important means of
production as well as the government in their hands, a
state of socialism would exist during which publicly
owned industry would gradually absorb smaller pro-

ducers. Such ownership in common would eliminate the profit motive, and the economy could be planned for the future good of society. With competition and selfish motives eliminated, everyone would benefit materially, and as man's material environment improved, so human nature would improve. The state, as policeman, would gradually lose its function and the dictatorship of the proletariat would fade away into a classless society. In this millennium, the final and perfect historical stage in Marx's mind, all economic and hence all related struggle ended. Man at last would be free to employ his faculties to the limit.

So Marx imagined the future with the absolute conviction of recorded history, but the obstacles were many. Parliaments, kings, and a czar ruled in Europe, all jealous of their power. In the East there was very little industry and hence no army of workers to raise revolt. During Marx's life, Britain, Germany, and France were the capitalistic strongholds, and here Marx envisioned his mission being achieved. But even at his own level of struggle, there was opposition and disunity. There were Socialists, less radical than himself, imagining peaceful change. These Marx dismissed with contempt. There were anarchists who, like himself, dreamed of a stateless society, but one very different from his. The anarchists simply planned to burn down the government where it stood. For Marx, there was no science in their fiery purpose, and he dismissed them, too.

Marx was a philosopher, not an activist. Apart from his writing, he undertook only one important organizational activity, and that was the leadership of the International Workingmen's Association, beginning in London in 1864. This group has since been referred to as the First International. It lasted twelve years and was a failure. The Second International was called together in 1889, after his death, and it lasted up until the First World War. Its blunt attack was concentrated

on the industrial West, and it ignored czarist Russia almost entirely. After all, Russia had few industrial
workers, only isolated peasants and a core of intellectuals stifling under czarist feudalism.

Russia, the Fertile Field

Czarist Russia was a vast, backward country overrun for centuries by the Tatars. It lay forgotten during the Renaissance and the Reformation that illuminated western Europe. Capitalism began flexing its muscles in England while feudalism still prevailed in Russia, but change began peacefully enough with a flowering of the Russian intellect. Tolstoi and Dostoevski were among the writers who complained of injustice to the masses. On March 3, 1861, Czar Alexander II, autocrat of all Russia, abolished serfdom. It was the right and honorable thing to do, but it came at the wrong time. The right time had long since passed. This mere taste of freedom, without the economic changes necessary to make it meaningful, created more discontent. And although the czar remained personally respected by the peasants, he became the target of one assassin after another from among the radical alienated youth. On March 13, 1881, a nihilist radical wounded one of the czar's Cossack guards with a bomb. Alexander mildly reproached the would-be killer as the police held him, and then he thanked God aloud for his escape. "It's too soon to thank God," shouted a second fanatic as he hurled a fatal bomb at the czar's feet.

Nicolai Lenin Alexander III, who had watched his father die, opposed all revolutionary movements and built up his police force. When a man named Alexander Ulyanov was hung for an alleged plot against the czar, his brother, Vladimir, a young man of twenty-one at the time, swore blood revenge. In time, he would change his name to Nicolai Lenin. He would have his revenge, not against Alexander III, who died peacefully, but against his weak and vacillating son, Nicholas II. As early as 1904, things were going very badly for Nicholas. He was losing a war to Japan, and unrest was simmering in Moscow. In the next year, a protest march resulting in bloodshed would be remembered as Bloody Sunday. All over Russia, the workers' councils, called soviets, which were to be so useful to Lenin in later years, began massive strikes. Government officials resigned, and anarchy reigned. Nicholas was driven to concessions. He agreed to a parliamentary government, although of the most limited type, and the following year the first national elections in Russian history took place. Russia seemed on the verge of surging forward peacefully into the twentieth century.

It was not to be. The tensions that make for historic change, by no means all of them Marxian, were building up in western Europe. Marx's *Kapital*, forecasting capitalism's fall, had long since entered Russia, passed by censors who considered it incomprehensible gibberish. Not so a young idealist, Georgi Plekhanov, who found it inspiring reading. In 1883, he left Russia for Switzerland, where he formed a group of Russian Marxian Socialists.

Meanwhile, Nicolai Lenin, true to his pledge, was preaching against the government. His efforts were rewarded with exile in Siberia. A few months after his term of exile had expired, he too went to Switzerland and joined the Russian Social Democratic party. At first he had deeply respected Plekhanov, but disagreement came after a short time. Remembering his brother, Lenin insisted on revolution led by a vanguard of revolutionaries. This was Lenin's first practical contribution to the Communist cause. He could not imagine the Russian working class as a whole spontaneously developing class-consciousness. He devised the idea of a hard core of elite, dedicated revolutionaries who would supervise and indoctrinate the workers while infiltrating decadent capitalist institutions such as the army and the bureaus of government.

This theory of the professional revolutionary bound to his fellows by military discipline appeared in Lenin's first really influential pamphlet, *What Is to Be Done?* published just after the turn of the century. The idea of the professional revolutionary constituted a real departure from Marx, who had devoted his efforts to developing mass trade unionism. By 1903 Lenin's doctrines had split the party into two factions. The Bolsheviks, literally meaning "the majority," followed Lenin. The minority, or Mensheviks, retained the traditional Marxian views. Among the Mensheviks was one Lev Bronstein, who preferred the name Leon Trotsky.

The Revolution   Heedless of the petty wranglings of minor eccentrics, Europe prepared for war. It came as a relief to Czar Nicholas, for patriotism mounted in Russia, and even the Socialists closed behind him. The Russian Army, however, was far from ready, and against the Germans it achieved one spectacular disaster after another. While the army sank into defeat and demoralization, the peasants at home were starving. Bread riots took place. In 1917 czarist soldiers fired on the protestors, and then the army began deserting to the people. The revolution had begun spontaneously and without leadership. Returning from the battlefront, Nicholas found his path blocked by revolutionaries, and in a railway car at Pskov he was forced to abdicate on the spot. A moderate government led by Prince George Lvov and Alexander Kerenski was formed, while far away in Switzerland Lenin hopped about in forgotten frustration. Only when the moderates in

power in Russia decided to continue the fight against
Germany did Lenin's chance come. He persuaded the
Germans that he would work to get Russia out of the
war, and for that purpose they sent him home in a
sealed railway car with the slogan "Peace, Bread, and
Freedom." On April 16, 1917, he arrived in Petrograd.

A moderate, bourgeois government was the last
thing Lenin wanted, and he took his Bolshevik doctrine
to the workers with another slogan: "All power to the
soviets." He didn't mean it, but the undisciplined workers and soldiers were susceptible to the persuasion of
demagogic slogans, and Lenin managed to disrupt
more conservative efforts at forming a government.
However, when an election was finally held to form a
lasting government, the Bolsheviks did badly. Lenin
took courage from Aristotle's doctrine, "Revolutions
are effected in two ways, by force and by fraud." He
found questionable grounds to ignore the result of the
vote. Since his elite was better situated and better organized than the opposition, he took control as though
the vote had been an endorsement. The following year,
1918, the Bolshevik party was reborn as the Russian
Communist party.

There was still substantial opposition, from both
right and left. The royal family had to be shot. The divided army fought among itself, but the Communists
occupied central Russia and had the support of the
peasants. While Marx had foreseen the emergence of
his ideal society in western Europe, where the proletariat would rise in an already industrialized state,
Lenin was absorbed by the great expanse of Russia, a
land dominated by peasant farmers. His determination
to harness them to the Communist revolution was his
second important addition to Marxian theory. By way
of incentive, he promised to give them the land of their
former lords.

Even with the mass of peasant support, the civil war
sputtered until 1921. Then the capitalist world, which
had given sporadic aid to Lenin's conservative opposi-

tion, wearied of the war. Russia herself was exhausted, but the progress of Communist consolidation could move ahead. It was a staggering task in a poor land, made poorer by more than six years of killing, but it was undertaken by bold, capable, and ruthless men.

In theory, the Marxian formula was to be followed, but where Marx had imagined a proletariat spontaneously conscious of its historic mission, he had never clarified what he meant by the dictatorship of that proletariat. Lenin had never had illusions about the ability of an amorphous mass of workers and peasants to generate a successful revolution. He had even less expectation that they could consolidate the results. So, into the formula "dictatorship of the working class," he introduced a substitution. "In behalf of" replaced the preposition "of." He might speak of democracy, but the immediate implication was far from traditional. The word meant to Lenin, at most, the mass participation of the Russian people. It did not imply free elections or the existence of more than one political party. It meant totalitarian socialism with himself at the top as dictator, administering the country through a central committee comprised of dedicated Communists down through a widening pyramid of party functionaries to the final cellular units.

In fairness to Lenin, he did not conceive of this governmental structure as perpetual. Rather, he regarded himself and his elite followers as a team of surgeons operating on a sick patient, Mother Russia. With the operation a success, the patient would presumably recover. The surgeons would withdraw, and Soviet Russia would experience the truly democratic life of the stateless Communist millennium.

Although problems within war-ravaged Russia were monumental, Lenin did not overlook the fact that the Communist revolution was a worldwide undertaking. Here, again, he modified Marx, who had concerned himself only with industrialized capitalist countries. Ironically, the backbone of the Russian Revolution had been the peasants. In other European countries, where factory workers were proportionately stronger, Communist revolutions had failed dismally. The implications would have been shattering for a strict doctrinarian, but Lenin was a pragmatic realist. If peasants rather than industrial workers rallied to the Communist banners, that was fine. With this in mind, it was Lenin who first enlarged the Communist world movement to include underdeveloped nonindustrialized countries where no true capitalism, and hence no class struggle in the Marxian sense, existed.

Leon Trotsky Lenin was not to live long enough to see how well this change in emphasis served world communism. Barely had the major industries of Russia been nationalized when, in March of 1923, he suffered a paralyzing stroke. Within the year, Lenin was dead. His obvious heir was Leon Trotsky. Trotsky was a university graduate, a dynamic and heroic product of the revolution, a man who had known the privation of banishment to Siberia. He had followed the Mensheviks during the early party split, rejoined Lenin in 1917, and created the Red Army while Lenin took over the government.

Joseph Stalin Like so many early Communists, Trotsky's strongest rival for power, Joseph Vissarionovich Dzhugashvili, went under an assumed name. Its English translation had a comic-strip tone—"Man of Steel." In Russian, it was "Stalin." Despite the name, this amiable, plodding party worker who always voted with the majority seemed no threat. Yet Trotsky and Lenin had never much liked the man, and before his death Lenin had been planning to have Stalin fired from his post of general secretary of the party on the grounds of "rudeness." This was revealed in Lenin's testament dedicated to his wife, Krupskaya, but Stalin suppressed the document and consolidated his power.

The son of a shoemaker, Stalin had been expelled

from a seminary for radicalism in 1899. He'd joined the underground under the name Koba (meaning "the indomitable") and had gravitated to the Bolsehviks in 1904. Later he became the editor of their official newspaper, *Pravda.* In the revolution he was unimportant, and no match for Trotsky intellectually. But where Trotsky was a theorist, Stalin was a dogged opportunist and organizer. Stalin was willing to take routine jobs that bored his colleagues. None of them seemed to realize he was building a fortress within the party through gradual control of the secretariat and various commissions, by systematically removing from office friends of Trotsky and replacing them with his own followers. Later Trotsky would comment in his book *Stalin:* "He is needed by all of them—by the tired radicals, by the bureaucrats, by the kulaks, the upstarts, the sneaks, by all the worms that are crawling out of the upturned soil of the manured revolution."

Apart from the sheer quest for power, the two men differed fundamentally on the future course of the revolution. Trotsky, the optimist, saw the revolution progressing democratically with the cooperation of the workers. Stalin, a bureaucrat by nature, lacked confidence in the regime's popularity. With the help of his allies in the politburo, the controlling executive committee of the Communist party, Stalin kept Trotsky from a commanding position.

Another issue between them concerned international communism. Traditionally the world movement came first, but Stalin insisted that Russia could build a Marxist society in Russia without the support of the proletariats of other countries. Trotsky clung to the traditional international emphasis, but his view became less popular as international communism in the 1920s met with no success. Must the Russian Revolution be dragged down by the failure of communism in other lands? Stalin denied it, and his was the brighter hope.

Trotsky was at first considered to be in error. Then he was viewed as a heretic, and one by one his offices

were stripped away. In 1927, he was driven from the
party. Hounded into exile, he moved from country to
country, ending up in Mexico. He was finally fatally attacked there on August 20, 1940, by Stalin's agents,
and died the next day. All who espoused Trotskyism
courted a similar fate.

While Marx had theorized the revolution and Lenin
had brought it about, Stalin was left to harvest its fruits.
He had the party and the machinery of government
behind him. The Communist party, regarded as the
vanguard of the working people in their struggle to
strengthen and develop the socialist system, has a monopoly of political power in Russia. Without a rival, it
still describes itself as democratic on the premise that
the elimination of class rivalry in Russia had eliminated
any need for diverse representation. Therefore the
party—made up of about a million members out of a
population of 194 million in Stalin's day and over 12
million from a population of 240 million today—holds
power over public policy and foreign affairs.

Ruling the party itself is the politburo. It, in turn, is
subject to the will of the general secretary, who was
Stalin as long as he lived. The party, of course, re-
quired governmental machinery. This consists at the
upper levels of a congress of soviets, called the Supreme Soviet, which administers legislative power
through two chambers. From its members is elected a
presidium under a chairman. Like the party, the power
structure is pyramidal, and it was subject in the final
analysis to Stalin's will.

Stalinization   For Marx and Lenin, the world revolution had come first. For Stalin, it was simply a tool to
serve the interests of Russia, which he intended building up into an industrial fortress and a strong nationalistic state. Where Lenin's "dictatorship in behalf of the
proletariat" had been strict, Stalin's rapidly became absolute. To make Russian communism succeed in a
watchful world of capitalistic enemies, the first need

was industrial power. With major industries already in governmental hands, Stalin had no need to depend on the growth of a free market. He owned the means of production, and he simply told the factory heads what and how much he expected them to produce. To this end, economic goals were set for a span of five years. This was the first of the so-called five-year plans, and Stalin ruled over its administration like Ivan the Terrible.

Lenin had already destroyed the power of private businessmen and landowners in order to create a manageable industrial army; but even Communist workers had to eat, and they weren't eating much. The peasant farmers, with nothing in the way of consumer goods to buy, were sensibly eating their own produce instead of selling it. During the early days of communism, famine had gripped the land. Half a million people had died, and Lenin had been forced to establish a new economic policy allowing farmers to keep the land they had appropriated from their landlords and sell the produce from it.

By 1928, agriculture was doing well, but doing so noncollectively, and Stalin needed more food for his factory hands. It was unthinkable to trade with capitalist countries for consumer goods that would have induced the farmers to sell their produce, and Stalin's government lacked the funds and the patience to negotiate with the peasants. The alternative, from which Stalin never flinched, was ruthless force. In the process, he even concocted a scapegoat for Russia's failure to move more rapidly toward paradise on earth. He insisted that all the fault lay with the more wealthy farmers, the kulaks, whom he labeled capitalists in disguise. In practice, a kulak was any farmer who resisted Stalin's new policy of agricultural collectivization: that is, the seizure of privately owned farms by the state, for the purpose of lumping them into larger state-run farms upon which the former owners worked as strictly supervised employees.

Collectivization reached its peak in 1939. Stalin had proved he could take away the land, but he could not make the survivors work. It was not until the mid-1950s that Soviet agriculture recovered. Meanwhile half a million farmers died by violence or starvation. Millions were deported to Siberia. Somebody had to work the mines there, and few would do it from choice. With industrialization still in the future, it was expedient to have a good supply of "state criminals." There were strange Communist heroes in those days. Typical among them was young Pavlik Morozov. Evidently young Pavlik had an unresolved Oedipus complex, for he denounced his father for saving out a little grain from the collective. The father received ten years in Siberia, and his son a statue in Moscow's Krasnopresnensk children's park.

Organizing the farmers not only accorded with proper theory, it also had the short-term objective of getting food to the factory workers. Industry moved ahead at a fantastic rate in preparation for the inevitable war against capitalism and the millennium to follow. It mattered little in the larger scene that hundreds of thousands in the Ukraine and Northern Caucasus starved to death, along with one third of the livestock in all of Russia. That was the price, and Stalin was prepared to pay it.

Many old comrades of the revolution, some who had loved Trotsky, others who were pure Marxists, objected to this process of Stalinization. Some may even have plotted against Stalin. It was enough that he thought so, and in 1936 he began the great party purge. Confessions, true or falsified, were extracted by force. One implicated many. Like some medieval witch-hunt, victims were found in one government department after another. The end finally came amidst the police themselves. Appropriately, the last victim claimed was the chief of police, Yezhov, after whom the purge, the *Yezhovshchina*, had been named in the first place. Literally thousands of top officials were executed in the last years before World War II. Stalin emerged supreme, without challengers, but in doing so he had violated another basic Communist rule. He had set the individual above the party, tying its fortunes to the life expectancy of one man rather than to the enduring corporate entity of communism itself. Not until after Stalin's death did anyone dare to point out this fact.

While the Yezhovshchina had strengthened Stalin within the party, it very nearly finished him and the rest of Russia into the bargain, for the army had been purged of its best commanders and totally demoralized. When Hitler attacked in 1941, Stalin's defeats dwarfed those endured by the czar twenty-seven years before. But the savagery of the German invaders turned many potential defectors into staunch patriots, and the vastness of Russia gave her time to rally. She had manpower and citizens with a deep love of their country. And the Communists made full use of nationalist feelings. Russia's new industry, together with foreign aid, particularly from the United States, gave her the weapons to resist. Her victories in the end were complete and Stalin survived the war, respected not only at home but around the world, as the good, benign "Uncle Joe."

The glow was quick to fade as discord arose between Russia and the Western powers over the partition of Germany, particularly regarding its capital city, Berlin. Communist subversion began to infect the nations of Eastern Europe. The United States countered with massive military aid to the countries in the West. In Korea, American soldiers fought hand to hand against their former allies, the Chinese Communists, and the warm global cooperation of World War II became the cold war of suspicion. Old Communist world dreams were reasserted, and Stalin breathed the air of vast power. Things had changed since the early days when he had been a hunted bank robber and political fugitive. Military expenditures mounted, atomic bombs were tested, and the world seemed once again on the brink of war. Then, suddenly, on March 5, 1953, the "Man of Steel" died.

Nikita Khrushchev No one man could replace Stalin. Malenkov, Molotov, and Lavrenti Beria, chief of the secret police, ruled together. The trio broke up in July, 1953, when Beria was removed from his offices, and on December 23 was executed. His police were demoted as a power, and in time the size of the labor camps was cut back. Less violent jockeying for power continued until Nikita Khrushchev stood alone. An old party hand, peasant by birth and in manner, Khrushchev brought with him an earthy charm and a return to the atmosphere of Pre-Stalin days. In an address that shook world communism to its roots on February 24, 1956, Khrushchev denounced Stalin for his "cult of the personality." He cited his crimes, such as the execution as counterrevolutionaries of 1,108 of the fewer than 2,000 delegates who had attended the seventeenth party congress. Communism would return to the methods of Lenin, he said, which involved persuasion and explanation.

Changes were quick to follow. Authority, at least among the 12 million party members—in a population of 200 million people—was decentralized. Concessions were made to the peasants, and Stalin's plan to place agriculture totally in the hands of state-run communes was revised. More consumer products appeared on the market. Even for dissident intellectuals there was more freedom, though critical novels such as Dudintsev's *Not by Bread Alone* were attacked, and Pasternak's *Doctor Zhivago*, which was to become famous and win for its author the Nobel Prize for Literature, had to be printed and distributed abroad. The steps toward liberalization were small, but at least they moved away from the complete totalitarianism of Stalin's day.

Internationally, change under Khrushchev was more dramatic. While Stalin had awaited inevitable war and the dying outburst of decadent capitalism, Khrushchev spoke of peaceful coexistence and control of the arms race. These overtures did not mean that he disavowed eventual Communist conquest—not at all. In fact, he widened the cold war. While Stalin had generally limited his range of domination to those lands which his armies could physically control, Khrushchev saw communism's victory being won through economic aid, persuasive example, and indoctrination. Africa, Asia, Cuba, South America, the whole underdeveloped world needed help and guidance, and, following Lenin's insight, Khrushchev was determined it should come from a Communist source.

Then on October 14, 1964, Khrushchev was out; neither tried, nor shot, nor imprisoned, but abruptly and completely retired, left to die in peace. The reasons were various: mismanagement of the Cuban missile confrontation, an economic crisis at home, and his own efforts to secure total political power. His violent vilification of Stalin was also no small factor, for it had disrupted Communist parties all over the world for whom Stalin had long been a god. It also cast discredit upon Russian communism in general, and upon Stalin's still-surviving associates.

This move against Khrushchev did not indicate a complete revival of Stalinism, but rather led to the prettifying of an unsavory and embarrassing past, which has recently been further glossed over by the appearance of a modest, fatherly statue of Stalin in Red Square. When some dissidents gathered there to protest any ceremony honoring the ninetieth anniversary of his birth, no ceremony took place, nor had one been intended. Disappointed, the protestors got into an argument, and a banner bearing Stalin's portrait fell to the ground. A poet, Anatoly Yakobson, who was near the fallen flag, was arrested, charged with behaving foolishly on Red Square, and fined ten rubles. One of Yakobson's friends commented, "We are delighted to hear of this law, for our group has always opposed foolishness on Red Square." Clearly, though, Stalin has reappeared, raising the question: Is he only a harmless ghost or is he reincarnated in the form of Leonid Brezhnev?

The Present Day　Leonid Brezhnev and Aleksei Kosygin are the two men who have taken over Soviet power from Khrushchev. Their personal impression is so dull it is difficult to remember what they look like. They are bureaucrats born of Russian socialism: industrious, unimaginative, discreet, certainly not fiery revolutionaries. They are very likely a mirror of the society that is emerging in contemporary Russia.

Internationally, caution has set the tone of recent years. The new soviet administration got off to a provocative start, with the arrival of Kosygin in North Vietnam in February of 1965 just in time for a severe United States air raid. Brezhnev would presently accuse the United States of using poison gas in Vietnam, and there was talk of enlisting Soviet volunteers to aid North Vietnam in the war. The volunteers did not materialize, and internationally the status quo has generally been maintained. Efforts have been made by the Russians to appease China as well as the United States. Strategic Arms Limitation talks have continued doggedly in the hope of limiting nuclear arsenals.

There are two schools of thought that attempt to explain this new conservatism. On the one hand, it is attributed to the United States and her friends, and their efforts to frustrate the USSR. Without this vigilance, communism might immediately surge ahead to new conquests. The other side says that, along with de-Stalinization, Soviet world ambitions have modified. In Russia, there is a deep skepticism. If our collective farms don't work, they ask, and our centralized industries have problems, should we recommend our system abroad? In keeping with this attitude was the popular joke of the early sixties after the poor wheat harvests, when wheat was purchased from Canada: "Why do we have the most brilliant farm experts in the world?"—

"Because they plant grain in Kazakhstan and it comes up in Saskatchewan." Under Stalin, making such a joke would have been suicidal.

Communism has never been a success in the agricultural sector in Russia. Collectivization, though not a total disaster, has been a disappointment. Industrially oriented Communists have apparently never understood that the prime desire of all East European peasants was to own their own land. Increasingly, more farm land is back in private hands or under looser state control. Industry, too, is undergoing change. In Stalin's day, there was a surplus of unskilled labor. Now such labor is short. People are more valuable, and the demands of a more complex economy force doctrine to give way to flexibility. Khrushchev did a great deal to break down the strict centralized control of factory management that had existed before.

To organize a workers' group in opposition to management or to contemplate a strike, activities central to formative communism, would still land a man in prison in Russia, but at least the individual has a chance of changing his job or of registering complaints through prescribed channels. These were dangerous, often impossible liberties during Stalin's day. Unfortunately this liberalizing trend has been too much for the conservatives Brezhnev and Kosygin, who have called for tightening of state controls, more ideological exhortation, and stricter work discipline. As yet, they have had very little success, and the Soviet economy is in trouble. Living conditions are poor. There are shortages of consumer goods that the people demand. Even if the leaders wanted to, they could not return to the Stalinist past, nor can they deny certain economic facts of life as Marx and Stalin tried to do.

For Marx, only labor created values. Therefore any factory profit above wages was capitalist exploitation, so invidious a term that any such profit appearing in Soviet factories was labeled "surplus value." The measure of a factory's success was not whether it achieved a profit margin in a market depending upon supply and demand, but whether it lived up to the "demand economy" set by the government. For each factory there was a quota: for example, 10 million bricks, or 1 million tons of locomotives. If the quota was not achieved, spies and foreign agents were blamed, and the managers were fired. To avert this, the brick factory might achieve its quota by suddenly changing over to smaller bricks, the locomotive plant to making ponderous, rail-crushing engines. Despite communist dogma, the absurdity of such occurrences and the logic of economics exert strong pressure toward decentralized control, a market sensitive to consumer choice, and success measured by surplus value (or profit) instead of simple output. Khrushchev was aware of these facts of economic life, but his successors, conservative doctrinarians at heart, have tried to put on the brakes to stop the change.

With the spread of education so necessary to an advanced industrial society, a new intelligentsia has been emerging in Russia. Although the present party bosses would hesitate to use guns against their striking workers, they have been heavy-handed in dealing with dissent ever since the brief flowering of freer literature under Khrushchev. Consequently a vast underground literature called *samizdat*, that is, "self-publishing," has been hand-typed and circulated. It has led to unrest and a response of tightening control. In 1968 several writers, among them Aleksandr Ginzburg and Yuri Galanskov, received prison terms of five and seven years for "upsetting" the Soviet community. In 1974 Alexander Solzhenitsyn, a writer of Nobel-prize-winning caliber, was expelled from the Soviet Union for his opinions. One may observe, after all, that this is a vast improvement; Stalin would have had the lot of them shot. But it is still far from the tradition of individual freedom and liberty accepted in the West. A most chilling method of dealing with such intellectual deviants is to pack them off to a mental home, wrap them up in wet canvas, inject them with drugs, and house them with the genuinely insane. Such frightening tactics are reminiscent of Hitler, Stalin, Czar Nicholas I, and many of the latter's predecessors.

For anyone accustomed to Western freedoms, the situation in Russia would be intolerable. Despite limited opportunity in choosing one's work, restriction on foreign travel to only the highest party members, the repression of religion and all forms of overt criticism of the regime, the Russian citizen of today can look back on a blacker past and say: We are not starving; no one will come to shoot us in the night. If nothing else, the Soviet Union has become a tyranny within the law. In general, the courts of the Soviet Union deal out fair and folksy justice. A man can be heard, even if now and then the laws are changed to raise the penalty after the crime has been committed, the sort of ex-post-facto law that would turn an American judge's hair white.

An example of the difference in attitude between the Western democracies and the Soviet Union, between the emphasis on the individual and his fulfillment as opposed to the fulfillment of the state, often at the individual's expense, occurs in Soviet Russia's so-called Parasite law. Under this law anyone who is not gainfully and usefully employed for the good of society may be uprooted from his home and sent to a specified location where work will be provided. Candidates for this administrative extralegal punishment include pimps and prostitutes and anyone who gets drunk regularly or works irregularly. There are merits in such a proceeding. How quickly the streets of New York City could be cleaned up by regimented vagrants! But there are grave dangers. What does a court define as useful employment? Does it include critical writers? Avant-garde painters? Or does it not?

Nevertheless, the Soviet Union has come a long way from the serfdom of just over a hundred years ago. A counterrevolution today is unthinkable. True, there is widespread discontent, but not so much because of the limitation of freedoms known in the West that few Russians have ever experienced. Rather, it is an unhappiness at the continued low standard of living, poor and limited housing, the unavailability of the material plenty that is known to exist in the West, and that might be more available to Soviet citizens if the command economy were directed away from enhancing a powerful state to providing its individual members with the comforts of life. There is little disloyalty. The people don't want to overthrow their government, they simply want more out of it. And at the top there is a very complacent aristocracy, not one established by birth and automatic inheritance, but by party devotion and ability.

Russians today still like to voice the old formulas of Marx and Lenin. They have reason for pride in the emergence of a great nation, and cause, too, for disillusionment with their ideology, which has become but a thin crust spread over a very large pie. In theory, they are a classless society, yet a ruling group has emerged within the institutional embodiment of the party, and what may be spoken of as the dictatorship of the proletariat is in fact the dictatorship of a new Soviet bureaucracy. Such government in the hands of official administrators who are free of the popular will is as un-Marxian as the profit motive in industry. The fact remains that from the point of view of income alone a vast gap is developing between the government officials, executives, and scientists on the one hand and the workers and peasants on the other. With a maximum income tax of 13 percent as against 70 percent in the United States, the net difference is wider and still widening in the Soviet Union, while in the United States the income gap has a tendency to narrow. Once again Marx has reason to turn in his grave.

The economic potential of the Soviet Union is boundless. Russia is a huge, underdeveloped country with enormous natural resources. The only real ques-

tion is whether her leaders will adhere to inflexible and
inhibiting doctrine in its development, or whether there
will be a slow drift toward a market economy and perhaps toward democratic socialism. As wealth increases,
so will individual expectations and demands upon the
part of the intelligentsia as well as the general public.
Such demands are not likely, however, to threaten the
structure of the Soviet state, for Russians have been
used to a tightly run bureaucracy since the days of the
czars. The intelligentsia will easily absorb the ablest
children of the masses without revolt or purge. Un-
questionably there will be a diminution in ideological
fervor.

Industrialization in Russia has already begun to
bend slightly toward Western methods. The process
may be very slow, and it will be resisted on the part of
entrenched and conservative government. But there are
already courageous spokesmen such as the hydrogen
bomb physicist Andrei Sakharov, who has published an
open letter criticizing quantitative and qualitative lag in
the Russian economy. He speaks of the second Industrial Revolution and calls it a Western phenomenon,
with particular reference to the computerized methods
of the United States. In his view, industry must be decentralized. Information must be exchanged internationally, or Russia will stultify in its plodding, unimaginative bureaucracy. The bureaucrats smart under such
attack, and lesser heroes than Sakharov might well be
put under psychiatric care for such statements. Who
will prevail? The bureaucrats, mouthing old formulas
and guarding a closed society, or the more modern intelligentsia, confident that Soviet Russia can flourish as
a more open society? Only time will tell.

Whatever happens, a complete return to Stalinism is
unthinkable. Brezhnev has been called neo-Stalinist,
but times have changed and Brezhnev could not rein-
stitute such a one-man tyranny if he wanted to.
However, he does have power to move his nation
forward or hold back its progress. The Soviet Union

has long been a model for communism around the world. It may remain so, but, though its power is unquestioned, its desirability as a model for emerging nations depends on its ability to keep up with the times. This adaptability seems lacking in today's Soviet leadership. Not only countries of Eastern Europe that are within Russia's direct military sphere of influence, but emerging nations groping for a way, ex-colonies still remembering an exploited past, underdeveloped countries seeking quick affluence—all today are giving Russian words and deeds serious appraisal.

The Roots of
International Communism

Before the Russian Revolution, communism had been a world-oriented movement. Marx himself had presided over the first International Workingmen's Association, with delegates coming to the meeting from many European countries. Another such international congress sputtered along from 1889 until World War I, urging on the struggle for world communism. Its achievements were minimal. Russia, of course, was communism's first real success, but war-ravaged Europe of the early 1920s saw other "Socialist" uprisings. In Hungary, had the peasants proved as manageable as in Russia, victory might have been achieved. In Munich a bloody revolt was easily crushed. In those days, if a Communist were asked, "For whom are you most willing to die, world revolution or Mother Russia?" the correct answer was "world revolution." Not for long, however; at least, not on the part of a Russian Communist. In 1919, while the Revolution still sputtered, the Third International was called. No longer a convention of workingmen, it was in truth the first Communist international convention. It adopted the name Comintern, and under this name Soviet Russia would manipulate Communist infiltration and subversion throughout the world for the next twenty-four years.

The Internationals   Although the membership of the Comintern was worldwide, clearly Soviet Russia called the tune. One year later, at a second world congress, it set out twenty-one strict conditions that Communist parties throughout the world had to accept or be banished from the movement. Typical are the following: to fight reformism; to form nuclei in trade unions and capture them from within; to seek peasant support; to promote emancipation of colonial peoples; to purge petty-bourgeois elements. Of vital importance was weeding out the non-Bolshevik Left, the "opportunists," as Lenin called them, who did not look to Moscow for direction.

During the 1920s, Communist parties throughout the world responded to the Soviet Union, accepting from the various international congresses more and more organization along Russian party lines, and fighting their isolated and generally unrewarded battles against the governments of their respective countries. All the while, fascism—the political system in which all power lies in the hands of a dictator whose purpose is the achievement of national or racial supremacy—was growing in Italy and Germany. In the latter country, the Communists were so myopically involved in undermining the Social Democratic party that they were completely unaware of Hitler and his Nazis until it was too late.

Alienation from the world community reached its peak during the years 1928–1933, when Stalin had cemented power at home and called for a hostile, disruptive effort abroad. Then, in a reversal, while at home Soviet Russia purged her kulaks and commissars, a brief sunshine fell on the international movement, with a new unity of purpose in opposing the growing threat of fascism. The idealistic days of the Popular Front were launched with the Seventh International Congress, which met in the summer of 1935. At it Russia announced the radical about-face to the other national parties. No longer were they to work against their governments. Instead, they were to popularize world communism as a patriotic, open, cooperative organization bent on resisting tyranny and oppression. The shift from subversion to cooperation left most of the delegates bedazzled at first, but, like the responsive puppets they were, they carried the news home. The about-face was achieved immediately, and in most cases with profound relief at the prospect of knitting together a divided loyalty.

The Spanish Civil War   The great test between communism and fascism was not long withheld. In the summer of 1936, a series of politically motivated murders in Madrid gave the final excuse to the fascistically inclined Spanish Army with the general support of the aristocracy and the Catholic Church, to revolt "in the interest of the Spanish people" against the shaky Republican government. An army coup in Spanish Morocco was led by General Franco. Quickly the rebellion spread to Spain. Most workers and peasants rallied behind the official government. Battle lines formed, and the first real revolution in Europe since 1919 was launched with all the Spanish ferocity that had once frightened Julius Caesar.

Fascist Italy and Germany plunged in with men, arms, and airplanes, on behalf of Franco. The Western democracies officially aided neither side. Russia, however, came to the aid of Republican Spain, where communism had been a weak and splintered party. Stalin had more than one reason for involvement. First, it was a chance to move the center of anticipated war far from his own vulnerable frontier. More obviously, it was an opportunity for the spread of international communism. While niggardly with arms, which he sent along only at a stiff price, Stalin generously sent out political advisers and military instructors, for it wasn't victory alone that he wanted, but a Communist victory. When Republican successes suggested victory through negotiation, Stalin saw to it that his Communist officers

initiated a disastrous and pointless offensive. Through
such tactics, Soviet communism gradually changed
what had been a Fascist versus Republican war into a
confrontation between fascism and an alliance of liberals, Republicans, and Communists that was dominated
by the Communists.

Japan was meanwhile mounting a threat to Russia's
Asian back door. Purges in the Russian party had
reached a bloody peak, and aid to foreign shores was
no longer practicable. Republican Spain, now politically divided by Communist manipulation, was left to
die and with it thousands of idealistic young "communist" volunteers from a number of Western democracies. Even the United States was represented by "the
Abraham Lincoln" and another brigade. This was the
naïve period, when to many, international communism
seemed to be the hope of the world. It was a period
that would not come again.

In late August, 1939, the ideological skies darkened
abruptly when Soviet Russia, the champion of antifascism for the past five years, announced a mutual defense pact with Nazi Germany. Suddenly the new enemies of communism were Polish landlordism and
British and French imperialism. The violent reversal
was too much for even some hard-core Communists to
take. For some of the survivors of the Abraham Lincoln Brigade and their spiritual cousins, it was the cynical end of the rainbow. Membership in world communism dwindled until the early summer of 1941, when,
suddenly, Germany attacked Mother Russia. Out went
the shock waves. In her peril, Moscow announced the
great patriotic war of democratic nations against the
Nazi tyranny.

World War II   International communism fell into
line once more, but the innocent dedication of the Spanish days had gone. For those to whom communism had
been an ideal dream, there would always remain the
disturbing memory of the Soviet-Fascist pact, but the

balance of the war served communism well. Disillusionment within Russia became submerged in patriotism, and so tremendous was her effort at self-preservation that the Soviet Union emerged from war a mighty world power. Communist-dominated resistance movements in Eastern Europe, China, and Indochina also prospered. Communist resistance fighters in East Europe emerged as patriots and heroes.

War cast a rosy glow on the Grand Alliance. In 1943, the Comintern was dissolved in form, if not in fact, and the illusion began to emerge in the West of democratic nations living in harmony under the supervision of a paternal United Nations. Such a hope was of short duration. With victory, the glow was quick to fade. Tensions developed, and in 1947 the Cominform replaced the Comintern as the guiding body for international communism. Superficially it concerned only the Communist-dominated countries of Eastern Europe and the promising Communist parties in France and Italy, but in fact its influence was very little changed from that of the Comintern. However, the Cominform achieved no more success than its predecessor, and in its turn it, too, dissolved. With the demise of Stalin, the intensity of rocket-rattling regarding the disposition of Berlin and the Korean War began to diminish, and it reached a new low with the Cuban missile debacle of 1962.

Khrushchev initiated a period of winning friends via massive aid programs to underdeveloped nations. This, too, has diminished. Apart from arming various Arab countries, this indiscriminate aid program has largely been replaced by more subtle and less costly diplomacy, in an effort to achieve small advantages without calling forth major reactions. One example of this new diplomatic approach has been the effort at rapprochement with West Germany.

The Russian drive toward world revolution, the old idealistic dream, has lost much of its luster. Soviet Russia now seeks primarily to consolidate itself as a world

power. Allies are no longer restricted to by-the-book
Communists, and to this end the Soviets have achieved
much success and many problems. Among the latter
are a lagging economy, a restive Eastern Europe, and
unstable Arab friends. The Kremlin, like the White
House, is haunted by doubts, not the least of which
relates to her most powerful and all-too-eager heir,
Red China.

Postwar Divergence   In Marxist theory, international
discord is caused by capitalist imperialism. Among
Communist countries, "fraternal peace" is expected. It
seemed to exist between China and Russia back in
1949, when Chairman Mao visited Moscow in the
hope of solidifying relations while at the same time
persuading the Russians to return machinery con-
fiscated from Manchuria during the war. Moscow
was agreeable all round, and Mao went home speaking
of the "eternal and indestructible" friendship between
the two countries. Traditionally, however, no matter
how repugnant to communist theory, there has always
been enmity between the two. In Russian eyes, China
has always represented the yellow peril as typified in
the popular joke about the Soviet and Chinese diplo-
mats who were discussing the latter's population problem. The Chinese diplomat suggests that perhaps it
might be solved by moving a few Chinese to sparsely
settled Siberia. "What do you mean by a few?" asks
the Russian. "Oh, perhaps 80 or 90 million for a
start," comes the reply.

Since 1949, the traditional fear and enmity between
Russia and China has found doctrinal channels. Of
particular importance has been the divergence of world
views. Russia came early to speak of competition
rather than conflict with the capitalist countries, while
Mao coined the slogan "Political power grows out of
the barrel of a gun." Until recently, Mao insisted on a
Communist hegemony achieved by violent means.
Now, through personal diplomacy involving a rapid

thaw in Chinese relations with the United States, the principal capitalist bogeyman, even Mao has modified his militancy.

A one-sided world, all democratic capitalism in the Western sense or all communism, achieved by either violence, subversion, or overwhelming competition, seems increasingly less likely. Islam and the Catholic Church, though once bitter enemies, have both sturdily survived centuries of crusading, and so undoubtedly will the opposed and evolving ideologies of the twentieth century. This is not to deny that communism has already made rapid progress, not so much toward the Marxist millennium as in terms of territorial control. It will be the purpose of the forthcoming chapters to evaluate the communism in that territorial spread, both in its theoretical and in its practical aspects.

European
Communism Today

Historically and philosophically, communism developed
out of Western European culture. There Marx confidently expected capitalism to run its violent course in
the leading industrial countries: Britain, France, Italy,
and Germany. No such revolution has taken place, and
it is now less likely to than when Marx was writing.
What went wrong with his plan?

Principally, Marx's theory that the advance of industrialization would lead to increased exploitation of
the worker simply operated in reverse. As industry
prospered, so did the worker. Communist parties still
exist in Western Europe, particularly in France and
Italy, but they are well-fed Communists. Their interests
are better served by labor union action within the community than by risking all on overthrowing society.
Furthermore, they have learned through bitter experience that international communism as directed from
Russia serves Russian objectives with complete in-
difference to local considerations.

The only chance that communism really had in these
Western European countries was during World War II.
As in Eastern Europe, the resident Communists in
German-occupied Italy and France were active in the
resistance movement with an eye to taking over the

government after the war. While the Western allies encouraged only minor sabotage and the preparation for a final uprising in support of the advancing armies of liberation, Russia exhorted the Communists to massive sabotage operations to take the pressure off herself by involving large numbers of German soldiers elsewhere. Such a provocative policy tends, through the escalation of hostilities, to force moderate patriots into extremes—in this case communistic loyalties. In Germany, where the Communist party had been very strong before Hitler's takeover, there was very little underground activity, and most of the Communist elements had been rooted out by the Gestapo. There was simply no basis left upon which the movement could flourish after the war.

The case of Britain is unique. There capitalism was born and there Marx wrote his anticapitalist books. The Communist party is still legal in Britain, but it has done itself more harm than good by its miserable showing at the polls. Superficially, this can be explained by the fact that the mass of British workers faithfully support the Labour party, which is vigilantly anticommunist. The real reason, however, is democratic socialism.

Unlike communism, this political theory was never based on violence, had neither a rigid plan nor a dogma, but rather relied on the motto "Reform without resentment." In the early days, the movement was led by a group of sober intellectuals such as George Bernard Shaw and H. G. Wells, who called themselves the Fabian Society. Devoted to democratic socialism, Britain's Labour party enjoyed a steady growth at the polls until it became the majority party. Many of its goals have been achieved, such as the nationalization of several major industries; the return of a Conservative government is not apt to occasion many backward steps. The success of democratic socialism and the failure of communism in Britain suggest that freedom is a better weapon against communism than repression.

Eastern Europe Eastern Europe is sometimes referred to as the "Communist bloc." It consists of East Germany, Poland, Czechoslovakia, Hungary, Yugoslavia, Bulgaria, Albania, and Romania. On the whole, these countries lagged far behind the rest of Europe industrially before World War II. None were Communist, but all except Hungary had Communist parties. With the war and the German occupation, resistance developed, and it prospered in the mountainous regions. Unlike most of the other resistance groups, the Communist fighters were already organized and had growing support from outside. Their successes against the Germans were more spectacular. They were not encumbered so much by local interests. If the Germans burned down a town in response to an act of sabotage, the Communists would have that many more displaced and embittered recruits. Conversely, the prospering local citizen with love of town and country would hesitate before bringing down such havoc, and in many cases he did not act at all.

In this way domestic communism was doubly strengthened during the war years. With the Russian occupation of Eastern Europe during 1945, local Communist groups emerged from underground. Only in Yugoslavia and Albania had the local Communists displaced the German Army, and this, along with strong nationalist feelings, had major implications for the future.

During the rosy glow of Allied victory, "Popular Democracies" were established throughout Eastern Europe. These democracies initially shared power among the bourgeois parties, the peasants, and the Communists. Gradually or rapidly, depending upon local circumstances, Soviet-backed Communists began to take over key positions in the lawcourts and amongst the police, so that by the spring of 1947 the coalition governments were giving way to absolute Communist control. "Salami tactics" was what Hungary's Stalinist boss, Mátyás Rákosi, called this gradual slicing away of civil liberties.

Never was the issue one of workers and peasants battling the bourgeoisie. The only question, except in the case of Yugoslavia and Albania, with their home-grown Communist governments already established, was the degree of cooperation with Moscow. With alternate threats of economic deprivation or the application of military force, if need be, it was Moscow that manipulated the situation from behind the scenes. While Stalin lived, the puppet states danced to his tune. With his death and subsequent vilification, many hard-line Stalinists were dismissed or held up to ridicule. Unrest was felt throughout the entire East European bloc, and in more than one case, as we will see later, revolution was attempted.

Nowhere did it succeed, yet nowhere has the near-monolithic structure of Eastern Europe been restored completely. Like a cracked ice floe, these countries continue to drift in the same current; yet they are drifting apart in the same way that the Western democracies, polarized around the United States after World War II, have increasingly become independent and learned to make their own decisions. Within this general context, the countries of Eastern Europe must be examined independently for national characteristics and details of geography, episodes, and personalities that have particularized them as individuals within the family of communism.

East Germany The DDR, or German Democratic Republic, is the only Eastern-bloc country born of World War II. Prewar Germany had had its Communists, but few survived the conflict. About the time Hitler, deep in his Berlin bunker, was putting a pistol into his mouth, Walter Ulbricht followed the Russian tanks into Germany from his exile in Moscow. This returning German was Stalin's disciple, and Ulbricht's original purpose was to aid the Soviet military authorities in their efforts to normalize civilian life in Germany. He arrived in devastated Berlin on May 2, 1945, and set about organizing an administration before the Western Allies could come and register complaints. At first, there was no sign of a Communist coup. In fact, Stalin must have been uncertain what course the future would take. The military occupation was regarded as temporary, and reunification with the Western two-thirds of the country was a possibility.

The eventual split, which began in earnest during the summer of 1948 with the Soviet land blockade of West Berlin, was as much a consequence as a cause of the growing cold war. That same autumn, East Germany's People's Council began drafting an East German Constitution and the German Democratic Republic was proclaimed in 1949, but not until 1952 did Stalin commit East Germany to the people's democracy that he had initiated throughout the rest of Eastern Europe. Then the usual process was applied. A local Communist party took orders from Moscow, and there was final amalgamation with and absorption of the competitive socialist party. Then Walter Ulbricht, a good Stalinist and leader of the SED-Socialist Unity Party, took over.

Times were hard. While West Germany was being rebuilt by Marshall Plan aid, Russia was making good on her demands for reparations at the expense of East Germany. What remained of East German industry was packed off to the Soviet Union. No rebuilding took place. Young people fled the country. With the pathetic resources available, Ulbricht set about organizing a "command" economy based on the Soviet model. The worker was elevated and idealized so that it became easier for a worker's son to get to the university than for the son of a professor.

One day Adolf Hennecke, a coal miner of the heroic John Henry stamp, became a hated national hero for digging 6.4 cubic meters of coal in a Zwichau mine. This was nearly four times the daily norm, which in consequence was dramatically raised. Such episodes, plus overwork and inadequate pay, led to increasing unrest until, in the spring of 1953, a general workers' strike began and spread. Higher wages and free elections were demanded. It took Soviet tanks to put a final end to the outburst, but during the 1950s one fifth of the native population of East Germany fled to the West. Curiously, it was this explosion of discontent that saved Ulbricht from being toppled by his lieutenants. Stalin had just died, and Ulbricht was a puritanical, doctrinaire Stalinist of the old school who had never defied the Kremlin in the days when his more idealistic colleagues were vanishing one by one.

Now, facing the workers' unrest, he defied Moscow's order for moderation and tried turning the Stalinist screws. If the dissent had subsided without Ulbricht's stern measures, Moscow would undoubtedly have supported his complaining subordinates, but such was the upheaval that Russia was obliged to give military support to Ulbricht's regime. When the trouble finally died down, he had weathered the storm and his erstwhile usurpers had been demoted. It must be said in Ulbricht's behalf that, though he emulated Stalin's ruthlessness, he was not equally merciless. His party purges were not accompanied by liquidation.

Though Soviet tanks had nipped revolution in the bud, they could not otherwise help the floundering DDR. It took time, determination, and an ugly symbol of totalitarian repression to turn the trick. Just after midnight on Sunday, August 13, 1961, trucks and tanks rolled into Berlin and began unraveling barbed wire. Two days later came concrete for a city-wide wall. Thus was sealed an escape hatch through which 160,000 East Berliners had fled the city in a period of seven months. According to Ulbricht, the wall was designed to repel "Western kidnappers and agitators," but clearly it had the purpose of keeping people in, not out. And it worked, far better than Ulbricht had anticipated. Not only did it keep people in, it destroyed hope for a better life outside. It forced East Germans to resign themselves to make the best of a bad situation, and they got to work.

The result has been an economic miracle. Of course, conditions in East Germany do not compare with the flashy affluence of West Germany, which had the industry to begin with, as well as United States aid to repair war damage. But the DDR has become in a few short years the eighth largest industrial power in the world. People live comfortably there, if not luxuriously. Nonessentials remain terribly expensive, but buying a television set ten years ago meant waiting two years for it to arrive at the store, at which point one had to pedal it home resting precariously on the handlebars of a bicycle. Now a technician will bring the set and install it on the day of purchase. In 1965, refrigerators were nine months back-ordered, but today they come directly, with an eight-day trial period. Nowhere in the Eastern Soviet bloc is the living standard as high as in East Germany.

Progress is the result of not only a different attitude, but of a change in economic approach. Under the old doctrinal command economy, the measure of success was quota, not profit. Results were often ludicrous, if not disastrous. A pajama-factory manager with a quota to fill but with insufficient allocation of material would progressively shorten the pants of the pajamas. A popular joke had two Chinese engineers visiting an East German factory and expressing admiration for what was produced there. "Very good, comrades—parts for elevators. We don't have them yet." Then, going too far, the Chinese ask, "What parts are they?" and receive the answer, "Signs reading 'Out of Order.'"

All that began to change under the direction of Dr. Günter Mittag, czar of East German industry. The DDR has gone further than its Soviet patron in shifting over to a decentralized system based on profit, even though the profit motive remains by definition at the root of all capitalist evils. Pure capitalism is not in the works, but a socialized network called the Vereinigungen Volkseigener Betriebe (Association of People's Owned Enterprises) covers many branches of manufacturing and distribution. In the more specialized areas, there still remains much private industry. Among the trades, about half of the shoemakers, watchmakers, plasterers, and electricians have joined cooperatives that offer a flat salary. At the price of losing independence, security is offered with the profits above salary being banked and given out as a dividend at the end of the year.

In the retail field, state-owned supermarkets are replacing the corner grocer simply because of convenience. In one area there has been backtracking toward more private ownership. When the state took over restaurants, cafés, and bars, the cherished German *Gemütlichkeit*—warm good cheer—went out of the establishments, and they were not patronized. Where the individual and the private touch serve the best interest of the state, it is no longer interfered with simply to please Marx or Lenin. The East Germans are too hardheaded and practical to let theory interfere with success so long as they do not feel the muzzle of a Russian gun at their backs.

To justify the "Democratic" in their official masthead, the DDR has faithfully held elections, each one preceded by massive rallies and ardent speeches. Until 1965, results were assured since the ballot carried only one slate of Communist candidates. Voters had to fill out this ballot under official scrutiny, and about the only possibility for a negative response was to boycott the affair. This could not hurt the candidates, but it might well imperil the voter's future. Then, in 1965, the list of candidates began to exceed the number of vacancies by about 20 percent. For example, for twenty available offices there would be twenty-four names. However, the names at the top were preferred, and the last four would not be elected even though their votes exceeded any of the first twenty unless the twenty received less than 50 percent of the votes. A small concession to democracy, admittedly. It has done very little to shake up the party structure, but it has done a great deal to put the candidates on their mettle. A defeat, a slight possibility for a preferred candidate, would be ruinously humiliating. Even a narrow margin of victory will put a dark cloud over that man's political future, and so campaigns are conducted with more frenzy than before.

East Germany today is the most prosperous and, after Bulgaria, the most loyal of Russian satellites. With a population of Prussian background, accustomed to authoritarian leadership, totalitarian socialism has worked well. Although many may chafe under the regime, almost all take pride in the results of their new socialized economic system. Prospects become ever brighter. The DDR is planning for the future with one of the best and most costly school systems in Europe. Seventy percent of her young people receive ten or more years of education compared to only 30 percent in West Germany.

Of course, the doctrinaire viewpoint is twisted. History is seen as the class struggle of the oppressed versus the exploiter, and the Roman gladiator Spartacus gets more attention than Christianity in a study of ancient Rome. The history of medieval and Renaissance Europe is presented as nothing but peasants rising up against their feudal lords. Not all of this is swallowed whole by an increasingly sophisticated student body, who learn the need to mimic but not necessarily to believe. Technically, in science and mathematics, preparation is excellent, and a resurgent DDR is moving smoothly into the computer age.

But a heavy price is paid. The DDR is a dull and oppressive society, its population of 17,096,000 dominated by 2 million energetic Communists who are omnipresent in even the smallest village. Only carefully selected foreign books can be found in libraries, and woe betide the student who speaks up in protest. Recently an exchange student received a seven-year jail sentence for "provocative criticism endangering the state." In fact, during a heated student debate, he had insisted that, without the presence of twenty Soviet divisions in the DDR, the regime could not be maintained. Foolhardy to speak out so candidly, but the implications of the punishment are staggering.

What of the future? One thinks first of the long-debated possibility of reunification with West Germany. Prospects are dim and growing ever dimmer. Almost a generation has passed. New loyalties have formed. The process of estrangement seems irreversible. It has been said, not entirely in jest, that before long shopwindows will feature signs reading, "East and West German spoken here." While the rift between Germany East and West continues to widen, there is a gap between the DDR old and new that may be as inevitable. Spokesman and pillar for the old ways was Walter Ulbricht. At seventy-seven he stepped down and his lieutenant Erich Honecker took over.

Ulbricht was in control longer than Hitler, and the state made undeniable progress under him. His successor is a reasonable facsimile who will move in the same firm, conservative, and essentially unimaginative direction. But there is a pragmatic younger generation hopeful of taking over. They are not revolutionaries, for they are confident of their achievements within their socialist system, but many have wearied of the dogmatic restraints of strict Marxism. To the new intelligentsia of DDR, the old rote phraseology that has served their elders demands editing. And whatever their pride of accomplishment, few can entirely forget the 856 miles of concrete slabs, bricked-up buildings, watchtowers, land mines, and yapping dogs that remain a tangible symbol of man's inhumanity to man. Some sort of change cannot be kept out forever.

Economically, then, East Germany has made a success of communism, adhering closely to the Soviet model. Recently a more pragmatic spirit has been revealed in a drifting away from the rigid social and economic patterns of the past. Whether democratic and humanistic progress can be kept out by an aging regime remains to be seen. Time, in the long run, would seem to be against it, though East Germany is a land accustomed to regimentation.

Russia's other European satellites appear to fall into two groups: in the North, the more Western-oriented trio of Poland, Czechoslovakia, and Hungary; to the South, the more remote area often referred to as the Balkans, including Bulgaria and Romania, and two Communist countries outside the Russian orbit, Albania and Yugoslavia. Beyond the obvious element of geographical location, though, the division has little merit. Physical proximity or remoteness from direct Russian military supervision naturally has been a factor in shaping the politics of these countries, but each has had its own unique history and evolution, and so we will consider them one by one, beginning with the three central European countries.

Poland　Geography cannot be ignored in the case of Russia's most northern satellite. Poland has had the historical misfortune of occupying ground between two strong, aggressive powers—the Teutonic and the Russian. Repeatedly over the centuries the land has been occupied by both Germany and Russia, and it was divided between Prussia, Russia, and Austria from the end of the eighteenth century until 1919, when it became an independent country. In recent times the aggressive powers have worn the guise of two expansionist ideologies, Nazism and Communism. Poland was Hitler's first target in World War II, and Stalin was also quick to take a slice of the pie. Before Russia had time to digest her section, Hitler seized all of the rest of Poland.

Throughout the war, the Polish government existed in exile, directing resistance from London. This resistance was intense and free of Communist infiltration, but it was removed at a distance. On Polish soil, Hitler unwittingly prepared the way for communism. With the beginning of the Nazi withdrawal, Polish resistance rose openly. The Nazis lingered long enough to destroy the flower of Polish patriotism. This bloodletting was achieved with the cynical cooperation of Moscow, which withheld its attack until Polish resistance had bled to death.

By the end of the war, the Polish people were decimated. The only source of power belonged to the Russian occupiers, who began their occupation by providing a committee of national liberation. By 1947, under a new "proletarian" constitution, the country had come under tight Soviet control. Heavy industry was nationalized along with most of the medium industry, wholesale activites, and retail trades. Not until the airing of Stalin's transgressions did opposition once more grow in Poland. In June of 1956, workers at the Zispo locomotive works began chanting, "We want bread." Riots ensued. Over fifty people were killed, but the rebellion never took as drastic a form as it did elsewhere that year, and it was quelled by concessions without need for Russia's physical interference. These bread strikes ushered in a period called "Golden October" under a new party secretary, Wladyslaw Gomulka. He had been imprisoned during the Stalinist era, and he arrived with the promise of dramatic reform. He kept the Soviet Army out by persuading Khrushchev that his policies would not deviate. This promise was sincere, for if he distrusted Russia, he hated Germany, and the Russian alliance made for security against the Teutonic foe.

The factors that make for individuality in Polish communism are many. Among the most obvious are her Western outlook and her traditional distrust of Russia, historically rooted in countless wars. Russia's cooperation with Hitler before World War II eradicated any possible illusions. There is more gloom than amusement in the joke that goes, "Comrades, for every boxcar load of meat we ship to Russia, we get a boxcar load of shoes . . . for repair."

A key to Poland's resistance is the Catholic Church, too strong to be uprooted. Over 90 percent of the population of the country are practicing Catholics. Most Polish Communist party members are nominal Catholics despite the theoretical incompatability of the two, and since 1957 religious instruction has been given in schools.

The present situation in Poland is by no means stabilized. Thus far, unrest has been channeled into strikes rather than resulting in revolution. Gomulka dismantled some collective farms and ostensibly diminished the secret police, but, under the label of eliminating political reaction, he sanctioned a final persecution of Poland's Jewish population. The hounding out of the country of these last few survivors of Hitler's death camps brought with it a revival of the secret police. Subsequently, an economic failure in 1970 led to a rise in the price of food and other necessities, with a corresponding drop in luxury prices. Many Poles interpreted this policy as "Let them eat refrigerators," and at the Gdansk shipyard workers attacked police with bicycle chains. Disturbances spread. Signs went up. "We are workers, not hooligans." Under pressure, Gomulka abdicated.

Edward Gierek became the new leader. Known as a pragmatist, he favored decentralized management and incentive pay. How his projects work out and how they are received by an independently minded public remain to be seen, but, as in East Germany, one trend is certain. Poland is moving away from the old communist ideology into a more functional form of communism.

Czechoslovakia Poland's southern neighbor, Czechoslovakia, was also used to Western ways before World War II. Industrialized, educated, and prosperous, her Communists were a respectable minority party before the war. Hitler seized Czechoslovakia by threat rather than force, and the later ravages of defeat did not touch her. However, the "liberating" Soviet Army was welcomed as a guarantee against Germany's age-old policy of *Drang nach Osten* ("push to the East"). The Nazi puppet government was overripe for the ax, and in 1946 Communists gained 38 percent of the vote. However, as the impact of the war faded, the popularity of Communist protection also diminished. The tide threatened to turn entirely in 1947 when Marshall Plan aid was offered, and the Communists had to work fast. Workers were armed and mass demonstrations organized. On February 25, 1948, without benefit of overt Soviet intervention, a coup took place. By summer President Beneš had resigned, but Jan Masaryk refused to surrender his post at the foreign office. He was found dead beneath his window. A Communist deputy succeeded him. Under the Communists a dismal and unimaginative rule was imposed, and Czech wealth and industrial know-how were drained to Russia.

In spite of the harassment of Czechoslovak intellectuals, the cultural life in Czechoslovakia eventually revived. It even intoxicated party boss Alexander Dubček, who began relaxing press controls and demoting hard-line Stalinists. Unlike Gomulka in Poland, he paid little heed to Russian rumblings. While Dubček's moves were a small threat to communism, they did question Moscow's dominant position, and on August 20, 1968, Party Secretary Brezhnev took action. For appearance' sake, he heard a cry of help from the Czech Communist party. Though Brezhnev alone heard this appeal, Soviet, East German, Polish, Hungarian, and Bulgarian troops went to the rescue. The Czechs awoke from dreaming to the rumble of Russian tanks. "Lenin, wake up! Brezhnev has gone mad!" appeared on many walls. Overwhelmed virtually without a fight, Dubček was drummed out of his official positions, but not murdered. Censorship and the old totalitarian ways returned, under the leadership of Gustav Husak.

Without this outside interference, Czechoslovakia would be on the way to being an independent Communist state, but the change had come too fast. The official government is now strictly subservient to Russian dictates, but below this crust the intellectuals, the students, and the discontented ones remain. As long as Chekhov's play *The Three Sisters* ran, the loudest applause was bestowed upon an actor watching the departure of soldiers from a small Russian town. He said only, "They left." The future can never be guessed, but of the past and the present this much can be said: of all the Eastern European countries under communism, the doctrine's application is least appropriate in Czechoslovakia, for communism's virtues lie in upgrading backward, undereducated countries; its vices, in restricting the individual. Czechoslovakia—the one Eastern European country with a democratic tradition and an industrialized economy—had nothing to gain from communism.

Hungary   Hungary is thought of in the framework of her bloody revolt against communism in 1956, but her struggle for freedom had begun long before that. Dominated for centuries by the Ottoman Empire and by the Hapsburgs of Austria, Hungary became, in 1867, an almost equal member of the dual Austro-Hungarian monarchy, and, as such, it took part in World War I, losing much territory to Rumania, Yugoslavia, and Czechoslovakia. In the hopes of getting some land back, Hungary joined Hitler: another bad choice, which left the country finally at Russia's mercy. The takeover was thorough, harsh, and Stalinist. Radical industrialization and collectivization took place. With Stalin's death, repercussions in Hungary were more violent than elsewhere, since a regime so closely associated with his policies had to be discredited.

With peasants assaulting collectivism and intellectuals demanding free expression, Imre Nagy took over the de-Stalinized government, granted concessions, and dreamed of drastic reforms. He was forced out of office in 1955, but by the early autumn of 1956 the pendulum of reform had swung out of the government's control. Students milled in the streets. Industrial workers met, demanding free trade unions. Then political police fired into a crowd. Fighting spread, and the Hungarian Army went over to the "freedom fighters." By the end of October, victory was close at hand, Nagy was reinstated, and the new government appealed to the United Nations for support. Their timing was unlucky. France and Britain had invaded Egypt in a blatant show of imperialism during the Suez crisis. Encouraged by this example and fearing a collapse of its own "colonial empire," Russia moved into Hungary with five thousand tanks. Thirty-five thousand Hungarians died in the hopeless fight while the world watched. Two hundred thousand fled to the West, and then the struggle was over.

With the champions of independence dead, imprisoned, or self-exiled, communism was oppressively reinstated. At this point, the country seemed doomed to the strictest form of totalitarian communism as a mere Russian puppet, manipulated by Moscow's hired hand, Janos Kádár. Time has somewhat modified this gloomy judgment, largely because of Kádár himself, who has proved to be no commonplace quisling. Despite strict control of the press, suppression of intellectual expression, and the presence of the Soviet Army, the outcome has been what some Hungarians call goulash communism. Shops are crammed with Western goods, and Count Basie has paid a visit. On television forums government officials can be questioned by phone, and some of the dreams of the 1956 revolt seem to be coming true. Collective farms have been granted more autonomy and, as with other Eastern-bloc countries, factories have moved from the old command economy to a program allowing sensitivity to Westernized free-market factors. Industrial development and planning have been decentralized, and priorities have been reorganized to emphasize agriculture along with heavy industry.

All this has come about subject to one absolute limitation. In Kádár's words, "It is impossible to be a Communist and at the same time anti-Soviet." Principally, this means subservience to Russian foreign policy, and Kádár's only deviations thus far have been in the direction of excessive zeal, for example, in his offer of volunteers to North Vietnam. For the time being, then, it seems that Hungary's foreign policy will mirror Moscow's. Domestically, the quiet revolution is likely to progress slowly within the limitations set by a vigilantly totalitarian government.

The Balkans   The Balkans are a largely mountainous cluster of countries, most of which are now Communist, that conjure up gypsies and guitar music. They are relatively foreign and remote, lost between East and West. Throughout history, this has been an area of perpetual political upheaval that in recent times has tempted great powers. Here modern states have been built out of the disintegrating Ottoman Empire, and the Balkan geographical divisions do not completely reflect the diverse cultures and ethnic minorities of the area. Though these countries have shared the ordeal of foreign overlordship, none feel comfortable together. Yugoslavia stands independent. Bulgaria remains loyal to Russia. Albania has become the enemy of Russia and the ally of Red China. Romania, the so-called Latin Island in the Slavic sea, craves Western culture and seems on the verge of quietly obtaining it.

Greece and European Turkey are also in the Balkans; neither has a firmly democratic government, but both are anticommunist and allied with the West. Only a fragment of Turkey occupies the Balkan peninsula, where it borders Bulgaria. To the East, beyond the Dardanelles, its longer and more sensitive Asian frontier faces the Soviet Union. These two have been enemies since the eighteenth century, and Russia's conversion to communism has done nothing to lessen Turkish distrust. Turkish involvement in the First World War cost the country the remainder of its European and Middle Eastern empire. The country's main objective in the Second World War was to stay out, though Turkish sympathies were with Germany. Only in February of 1945 did Turkey declare war against the Axis in order to qualify for United Nations membership.

Though the Soviet Union would dearly love to command the strategic area that Turkey occupies, she is not likely to do so. Turkey's noninvolvement in the Second World War made Communist guerrilla subversion impractical, and unswerving Turkish vigilance against all things Russian has not permitted Moscow to get its toe in the door. Recently, Turkey has been experimenting with Western-style democracy, but the real power in the country remains with the military. The resulting instability makes for political unrest, but at the moment communism seems a very unpropitious direction for that disconent to take.

Greece, until recently, was ruled by soldiers, though past events created a setting similar to that of her Communist neighbors. Resistance to Germany divided Right and Left as it did in the other Balkan countries with the exception of Bulgaria and Romania, which took the German side. The Communist guerrillas prevailed in Greece before the war ended, and would undoubtedly have controlled the country afterward had not Churchill ordered the landing of British troops at Piraeus. Not only was Greece far from the Russian frontier; it alone had emotional importance for the Western Allies as the democratic cradle of civilization. When the British finally exhausted themselves in the attempt to preserve Greece for the West, the United

States stepped in with massive aid. When Yugoslavia became involved with Russia, the Greek frontier was closed to Communist infiltration, and by 1949 Greece had been saved from communism. Civilian government, after a period of seven years of military dictatorship, was restored in 1974.

Otherwise, throughout the Balkan peninsula communism was methodically successful after the war. Where the governments had allied themselves with Hitler or been forced into humiliating capitulation, they were easy prey to Communist subversion. Totalitarian regimes were instituted, shaken and then modified along more pragmatic lines after Stalin's denunciation. About more than this, it is hard to generalize, and it is the differences in these countries rather than the similarities that deserve exploration.

Yugoslavia Though Communist, Yugoslavia and Albania stand apart from Russia's Balkan satellites. In many ways, Albania is a negative image of Yugoslavia; in Khrushchev's scornful words Albania is "a place for goats." But Yugoslavia has unequaled importance as far as the development of world communism is concerned. As a matter of geographic, not sociological or political, convenience, Yugoslavia was created after World War I by lumping together Serbia and Montenegro with former Austro-Hungarian lands of the South Slavs. The result was unworkable. Hostile Serbs and Croats, Catholics, Muslims, and Orthodox glared at one another under the rule of Serbian kings. In 1941 the army ousted the pro-German regency with the cry, "Better war than the pact," referring to a nonaggression pact that had been signed with Germany. The price of opposition to the pact was blood. Official resistance was crushed by the Germans in a week. Though elements of the army kept together under the right-wing leadership of Draža Mihajlović, his following was limited.

By 1943, the Communists were the only effective force in Yugoslavia still resisting the Nazis. They had begun as 12,000 men, but only 3,000 of this nucleus survived the war. Their slogan was "Brotherhood and unity for all Yugoslavs," and their appeal was limited to no single ethnic or religious group. Despite terrible casualties at the hands of the Germans, by the war's end their fighting force had grown to 140,000. Their leader, Josip Broz, known today as Marshal Tito, emerged a shining national hero.

During World War I, Tito had served in the Austro-Hungarian army. Taken prisoner, he had been trained as a Communist in Russia, and he returned to head the party in Yugoslavia as early as 1937. During the war, he had won his own battles and the final victory without Stalin's help. Thereafter, Tito went ahead to found the Federal People's Republic of Yugoslavia, a Communist state that he fully expected would outstrip Soviet accomplishments. Russia was delighted. More Stalinist than Stalin, Yugoslavia thumbed its nose at the United States and shot down her airplanes. Police terror reigned. Collective farms were set up, and complete faith in Marxist doctrine gave over the economy to heavy industry with no concern for the consumer.

The Marxist romance between Yugoslavia and Russia did not last long. Stalin was used to having his suggestions carried out to the letter, but Tito, too, was a hard fighter of the old school. In a letter to Stalin he said that no matter how much he loved the land of socialism, meaning Russia, he could not love his own country less. To Stalin, the implication of this honest patriotism was heresy. He began proclaiming "Titoism" as the disease of "National Communism." Tito retracted nothing.

In Yugoslavia, June 28 is a day full of portent. It is not only Saint Vitus' Day, a national saint's day, but also the anniversary of "The Field of Blackbirds" when, in 1389, Turkey had extinguished Serbian independence. More important still, it was the occasion in 1914 for a Bosnian youth to kill Archduke Franz Ferdinand, thereby precipitating World War I. On this date, June 28, in 1948, came the announcement that Yugoslavia was expelled from the Cominform. Invasion was anticipated.

Yugoslavia was helped by geographical remoteness from Russia; Soviet restraints mainly took the form of an economic blockade. Tito was forced to look Westward for aid. While doing so, he began to rethink political philosophy. "We are searching for our way," he said. With Stalin's passing, Khrushchev tried to make amends. He blamed the quarrel on Stalin, saying, "Our countries are linked by ties of long brotherly friendship and joint struggle." In so doing, he acknowledged a kind of independence on the part of Yugoslavia, a new posture that did not go unnoticed in the other Eastern satellites.

Regardless of this rapprochement with Russia, Yugoslavia had found its own way by this time, and that way will probably always be referred to as "Titoism." In agriculture, Tito was afflicted after the war with the Soviet tractor obsession. One must free manpower for industry. In Marxian terms, the goal had been to destroy the pillar of the old society, "the peasant," and replace him with the salaried farmer. By 1948, collectivism was going full blast, but its first five years were a disaster. In 1953, the ex-peasants were told they might leave the collectives. They left, preferring to start again from scratch.

Heavy industry has always been the Marxist key, and Tito tried at first to fit it to the Yugoslav lock. He tried so zealously that he recruited workers from the farms until there were great pools of industrial unemployed. When rejection by the Cominform forced him to look to foreign markets, he accepted the doctrine of supply and demand in order to survive. Workers were given new incentives such as shares in their factory's profits, and they were allowed workers' councils with their own elected leadership.

Today Yugoslavian borders have been opened to easy coming and going, and there is an air of prosperity in the land. One has the inclination to reflect upon the plucky little country that told the USSR where to get off, the perfect example of freedom-loving patriotism. That independent stature is fine as far as it goes, but politically Yugoslavia remains a one-party totalitarian state. The party itself is free internationally to go its own way. It can condemn Communist China or Russia as it chooses. It has been more moderate than most Communist countries in attacking the United States on its Vietnam actions. But let a writer, even a good friend of Tito's such as Milovan Djilas, suggest the introduction of a multiparty government, and that man risks jail for defaming Yugoslavia's Communist society and fomenting national hatred. Mihajlo Mihajlov is another important writer imprisoned for three and a half years by Tito. The Yugoslav citizen has certain freedoms, but he does not live in an entirely free society.

What follows Titoism? The question is important and must soon be answered, for Tito is an old man. He has great personal magnetism and his "personality cult" keeps the crowds chanting, "Tito is ours, we are Tito's," and the children singing, "Tito, Tito, little white flower, beloved by all the youth." After Tito fully steps down, will the old ethnic rivalries renew and tear the country apart as they have before? Probably not. Tito, at eighty, has proposed for the future a "collective presidency" of the two or three best men, each from one of the nation's republics. Already much of the administration and detail is in other hands, and if these men can work together, harmonizing the interests of the groups they represent, then Yugoslavia would seem to have a bright and prosperous future.

Bulgaria There remain three Balkan countries—Bulgaria, Albania, and Romania—to be touched on, and all three have uncertain prospects. They are all small, unlikely to shake the world. To begin with Bulgaria: it is poor and primitive, and too seasick from being a pawn in international struggles to want to rock the boat. In Bulgaria, Russia has long been accepted as a protection against Turkey on the one hand and the old Western enemies on the other. At times, a Bulgarian will joke about Russia. During the Chinese-Indian border dispute, both sides were using Russian arms, and it was said in Bulgaria that for this reason the war would go on forever, since nobody could win with Soviet weapons. A mild joke, but seldom whispered in official Bulgarian circles where one can be jailed for up to five years for simply leading "an idle, parasitic way of life."

Albania Khrushchev was undoubtedly correct when he said that there are more goats than people in the Albanian population, and an Albanian takes pride in the statement that "God must love Albania since it has changed so little since the Creation." During the war, resistance to Italian and German invaders polarized Left and Right as it did in Yugoslavia. Characteristically, the Communists prevailed. Fearing her neighbor, Yugoslavia, more than the remote Soviet Union, Albania started out as Russia's slavish disciple. However, when Tito and Khrushchev began their courtship, Albania's boss, Enver Hoxha, a former schoolteacher and guerrilla leader, protested. He feared that his country might become a wedding present to Marshal Tito. On one occasion he complained to Khrushchev that the Soviet rats were being better fed than his people, to which the Russian leader replied, "You have emptied a pail of manure on my head." Until this time, China had meant very little to Albania, but with the Sino-Soviet split, Albania could find some comfort in supporting Chinese policy. Where they had once addressed Tito with "We and the Russians, 200 million," now it was, "We and the Chinese, 650 million."

Albania has attempted to solve severe racial and religious unrest by means of murder and forced immigration and has effected a strong program of collectivization in both industry and land. Recently, the tumult and the shouting have died down. Yugoslavia seems content without her neighbor's goats, and a long-term bond between Albania and China, apart from a means of jabbing Russia in the ribs, seems hardly likely. Of late a few tourists have been allowed into Albania. Long-legged Scandinavian girls have begun a summer invasion that may in time work more changes than Tito's tanks, for Albania is a land poised between the sixteenth and the twentieth centuries.

Romania   Lastly, there is Rumania, calling itself in recent years Romania. There is some significance behind this one-letter alteration in the country's name, which came about officially in 1966. That period brought an easing of civil restraints and new independence in foreign policy to Romania, shown for example in the failure to condemn Israel as did the other members of the Warsaw Pact, a mutual defense treaty signed by the Soviet-bloc European Communist countries in 1955. The changing of Romania's name is a reflection not only of nationalist assertion but of a claim to a Roman background. At one time, the country was conquered and settled by Romans, and the ethnic strain is still present, so that the Romanians can claim some connection with Latin Europe.

Before the Romanians became involved in World War II, Russia had grabbed off a large chunk of Romanian real estate called Bessarabia. With Hitler's help, the Romanians took it back. By 1944, however, the handwriting was on the wall. The old profascist government collapsed, and backed by Soviet tanks, communism took its place. At first Romania stepped reluctantly into line and went about building up its economy with the usual concentration on industry. Until this time, though rich in oil, the country had been little industrialized and rapid growth was facilitated by the lack of old equipment.

The economy leapt ahead until 1962, when to counter Western Europe's Common Market, Moscow revised its own plan, Comecon, to accommodate non-European membership. In Russia's view, the economic progress of the entire Communist camp lay in the coordination of production, a kind of socialist division of labor. At the same time, Russia often took what she wanted from satellite countries, with no repayment. Under Comecon, Romania was to become the source of raw material for the Communist states. From the beginning Romania balked, preferring the theory that each Communist country should develop its own economy. Naturally, as this made for independence and competition, it went counter to Russia's desire to dominate the entire group of countries. For the first time, largely thanks to Romania's adamant stand, Russia was forced to abandon a major policy line.

Since then, Romania has progressed independently and rapidly, with an annual growth far exceeding that of any of her neighbors. For success, of course, outside trade is necessary, and Romania has never been loath to look Westward. Under Communist party boss Nicolae Ceausescu, head of the party since 1965, Romania has walked a tightwire. The summer of 1968 was one of near disaster. Less outspoken in its innovations, Romania had gone as far or farther toward independence than Czechoslovakia. At that time, the so-called Brezhnev Doctrine, justifying the invasion of Czechoslovakia and presumably any other state where the Communist system was endangered, was formulated. Romania protested, but kept its voice low, fearing the worst. Soviet troops did not appear, and Romania has been left to go its way.

On the other hand, President Ceausescu has visited both Peking and Washington, D.C. President Nixon in turn visited Bucharest. Romanian universities have been granted increasing autonomy and have sent the first scientific delegation from a Communist country to visit the American space program. On the other hand, keeping a balance, Ceausescu has not openly crossed the Soviet Union in international politics, and he has maintained a severely one-party system with strict controls on intellectual expression. Thus far he has gotten away with his balancing act, and with the bright economic prospects ahead for his country, he can depend on a docile population for some time to come.

To sum up briefly on the East European Communist bloc: in all these countries, communism was established as a result of World War II where formerly it had been represented by minority parties. Once instituted, communism adhered for a time to the absolute Marxist-Stalinist mold. Industrial growth was emphasized, usually with some success, particularly before the classic demand economy gave way to a more pragmatic market economy. In all cases, the firm adherence to older principles received a jolt with Stalin's death and subsequent denunciation. At this time it became clear that the dogmatism of the past had not permitted progress in the Eastern European countries. In a few cases, notably Hungary, the reaction went too far, resulting in abortive revolt and harsh consequences. But even in Hungary, a slow drift toward leniency has been renewed, and there has been a certain extension of freedom, particularly in the completely private sector. Where political criticism is concerned, all the governments of Eastern Europe have remained harsh. All remain one-party, totalitarian Communist, in part through conviction, in part through fear of Russia. Most remain subservient to Russia in the international field, the exceptions being Yugoslavia, Albania, and Romania, where communism has become strongly nationalistic. Yugoslavia, in particular, is an example that Communist states of the future are likely to follow.

China, the
Eastern Colossus

Massed red banners, echoing loudspeakers, gigantic posters of Chairman Mao Tse-tung; an Orwellian caricature not quite real; the red horde, as genuine and uncontrollably dangerous as nitroglycerin: such are the Western stereotypes of Red China. To the Soviet leaders, the pictures are not very different: arrogant, ungrateful upstart; perverter of Marx and Lenin; destroyer of Communist world unity; resurgent nightmare of the Mongol scourge. How did the moribund starved dragon of the opium dream revive so terrifyingly in less than fifty years? The answer is, of course, communism, creating with austere and selfless dedication what emperors for eons past never could: a single-minded purpose felt right down to the lowliest rice-paddy peasant. The facts are indisputable. The fair questions are: How? At what price? And most pressing, to what end?

No nation on earth has stretching behind it such a long, continuous history as China. The Shang dynasty can be traced back to before 1700 B.C. As one dynasty declined, another rose to replace it. Art and literature reached a high point under the Ming emperors, accompanied by a dangerous contempt for the surrounding barbarian world, a contempt that persevered and grew with the Manchus from 1644 to 1912. Until about 1750, because of famine and disease China maintained a relatively small and manageable population of about one hundred million people. Then, with new medicines and drought-resistant crops, the number of people tripled within fifty years. The Manchus began to lose control of the situation; they arrogantly ignored industrial change in the "barbarian world," and they were helpless when British traders, bent on economic exploitation, began bringing opium into China. At first it was a trickle, then a debilitating flood. Junks armed with archers were no match for Western gunboats. Britain first, then other nations took over the exploitation of China and forthwith set in motion the biggest drug problem the world has ever known. As the emperors lost stature, the inevitable contagion of Western ways bred revolutionary ideas and encouraged powerful warlords to independent conduct.

The Kuomintang Finally, in 1911, a bomb cached in a revolutionary headquarters accidentally exploded. Manchu officials, in behalf of the boy emperor, Hsüan-t'ung, began making arrests. Rebels fought back, and in Denver, Colorado, a thirty-four-year-old Chinese doctor who had been raising funds for a Chinese revolution heard the news and headed home. Sun Yat-sen arrived back in Shanghai on Christmas Day. By then all of South China was in flames. Within a year, he would emerge as leader of the Kuomintang, "the National People's party," and he would be the first president of the Republic of China. The republic was more of a phantom than a reality, and although the powerful general Yüan Shih-k'ai was president of the republic for a short period, he perverted the aims of the revolution. After his death assorted warlords were in control. In 1922, they hounded Sun Yat-sen out of Canton and onto a gunboat, where he met a young officer, Chiang Kai-shek. Within three years, Sun was dead and Chiang was left to continue the struggle against the warlords. The real contest was about to begin.

As early as 1918, at Peking University, the librarian had set up a society for the study of Marxism. China had always honored intellectuals, and there were communistic elements in native Chinese thought, so the new philosophy was well received.

In 1921, the Chinese Communist party was founded. As long as the new party was weak and the Kuomintang had warlords to fight, the two political groups were able to cooperate. Russia, still consolidating its own revolution, could offer little real support and was divided as to whether to back the Chinese Communists or the Kuomintang. The Kuomintang, at least, seemed to have the strength to break down local feudalism and prepare the ground for the greater class struggle to come. By the late 1920s, Russia was better able to support revolutions abroad, and she called for such a response from parties in other countries. In 1927 a small group of Chinese Communists, traditionally oriented toward the urban worker, launched the "Autumn Harvest Uprising." Support was not forthcoming. This Communist group, led by Mao Tse-tung, fled to sanctuary in the country, then to the mountains in southern Kiangsi. Recruits came: mutinous soldiers, bandits, and dispossessed peasants. Industrial workers were scarcely represented.

The Long March Meanwhile, Chiang had quelled the warlords, and in 1930 he introduced his "bandit-extermination campaign." The "bandits" included the Communists, whom he hoped to starve out of their lairs with a blockade that he set up in 1933. Chiang was nearly successful. At the point of starvation, however, 90,000 Communists and "bandits" broke through the Kuomintang encirclement and started on a flight of some 6,000 miles that led across twelve provinces, through forests and miasmic jungles, and over eighteen mountains. Battles with the Kuomintang were frequent, but some 20,000 Communists went all the way. They escaped not only Chiang's pursuit but also, though they might not have realized it at the time, Russian-dictated communism.

The heroic trek had diminished their numbers, but it had given the survivors fierce loyalty and confidence, together with a charismatic leader, Mao Tse-tung. No city-born, worker-oriented, traditional Marxist, Mao came of peasant stock, and he had been reared by a mother who was a devout Buddhist. Throughout the Long March, he had kept bright the new faith, and he had done it without benefit of Communist workers or Russian aid. He had done it with farmers and the dispossessed of the countryside.

The Chinese Communists might still have been overcome, but for the anticipation of the invasion of China by Japan. Moscow called for a popular front against the Axis. Mao and his diminished band, who were about to be finally gobbled up by the Kuomintang, called on Chiang's pursuing generals to unite with them against the Japanese. Though Chiang doggedly regarded the Communists as his prime enemy, his subordinates regarded internal politics as less of a threat than the foreign foe. They made Chiang a virtual prisoner and forced him to accept the united front against Japan. Tacitly united again, the Kuomintang bore the atrophying brunt of the Japanese attacks. Meanwhile, the Communists shouted patriotic slogans as they recruited and consolidated for the inevitable struggle to come. By the war's end, the Kuomintang was impoverished and depleted, while the Communists rode the crest of the victorious wave. A pretense of mutual goodwill was maintained until 1946, mainly for the sake of United States support. Then the final struggle began. Within two years, mainland China was in Communist hands.

The People's Republic   China suffered difficult and severe social problems: corruption in politics, chaos in economics, and ignorance, illiteracy, and superstition on a staggering scale. The appeal of the new People's Republic that the Communists had declared was immense. For the long run, of course, a millennium was promised in the Marxist-Leninist form: abolition of class distinction, affluence, the withering away of the state. But unlike in the traditional workers' revolt, the task in China fell to the peasants. Initially, with only five million avowed Communists, the existing Chinese government had to be kept functioning. Foreign businesses were at first tolerated, then exploited. The usual procedure was to force the businesses to employ larger and larger labor forces at higher and higher wages. The anticipated result was bankruptcy, with the benefits falling into the workers' hands and the failure vaguely attributable to sabotage on the part of the foreign companies themselves. Even such superficial tolerance of foreign investment vanished with the Korean War. Then the counterrevolutionaries were hunted with the so-called three-anti drive against corruption, waste, and bureaucracy. This drive was followed by a five-anti drive against tax-evasion, bribery, theft of state assets, use of knowledge of state economic projects for private gain, and misuse of labor and materials. The ill-famed "mitrailleurs of Lyons" of the French Revolution saw 2,000 executions. In Kwangtung Province alone, by the end of 1951, 28,-000 people had been put to death, but Mao was getting results.

Mao Tse-tung   For half a billion Chinese, Mao was Marx, Lenin, and Stalin rolled into one. His little red books, *Quotations from Chairman Mao Tse-tung,* guarded and studied like Holy Writ, is actually a simplistic effort to bridge the gap between West and East: between European Marxism and the realities of China. His principal contribution to communism, of course, was the innovation of a rural, guerrilla-type Communist revolution as distinct from that based on worker-oriented urban cells. Lenin had contemplated such possibilities and had made use of his peasants, but it took Mao to demonstrate conclusively that it is in the backward agricultural areas of the world today, not in the highly industrialized, that the communist appeal is likely to be most effective.

Of more limited importance is Mao's concept of political indoctrination based on the Chinese intellectual tradition of Confucian mind-training. It is this approach that has led to the endless posters and banners, the loudspeaker announcements, the "struggle meetings," and the tortuous process of *cheng-feng yun-tang* (self-criticizing rectification campaigns), all aspects of the movement that, taken out of context, make Chinese communism appear bizarre and ludicrous to Western observers.

It was in large part, too, because of Mao that the rift between China and Russia developed. With two such giants, both victorious in their own right and with a history of mutual distrust, discord was inevitable, but, in the early fifties, Mao could still speak "with love" of the Soviet Union. He needed aid badly then.

The actual rift came with the fall of Stalin and the denunciation by Khrushchev of Stalin's cult of personality. Mao by implication was included. He began calling Khrushchev a "psalm-singing buffoon," and the Soviet premier, never at a loss for words, described Mao as "a worn-out boot fit only to stand in a corner." Less openly, Khrushchev went on to explain that communes, the basic unit of Chinese communism, didn't work. "We tried them right after the revolution," he said. By 1960, Russia withdrew her aid from China and as a result became the scapegoat for all Chinese economic woes.

Two years later, she continued sending aircraft to India during that country's clash with Red China. There were disturbances along the Sino-Soviet border, and war between the Communist giants seemed imminent in 1969. China could only be the loser, at a fearful cost to the Russians, and she began casting about in the mid-sixties for other friends. While Russia had begun endorsing coexistence with the West and the making of allies through aid, instruction, and example, China called this approach revisionism and a betrayal of the people's war. Superficially, at least, Mao clung to the inevitable-war-with-capitalism theory. Thanks to his own military weakness, it was like threatening the local bully with a big brother, but the Soviet Union had no intention of playing that role. Nevertheless, Mao pressed international objectives along subversive and revolutionary lines.

The Great Leap Forward   During this unsettled period, Red China tried her "Great Leap Forward" and nearly broke her political neck. In 1957, Russia seemed to be prevailing in the space race. The United States was sunk in recession. China had to do something toward the apparently imminent Communist world victory, and so she announced that she was initiating an economic and social reorganization of sweeping proportions that would move China directly into a genuine Communist society without going through the intermediate socialist stage. Rapid industrialization was the objective of the new program, and it was to be accomplished through an expansion of the commune system. China implied that she was well ahead of Russia in communization and she was now about to leap out of sight.

This broad jump was to be largely the task of the peasants. They had already presumably taken a hop and a skip. The hop had come with the redistribution of land between 1950 and 1952. More prosperous peasants had been classified by the Communists as landlords, and most of them, particularly those who rented land, that is, exploited others, were eliminated, and their land was divided among the lesser peasants. There were 300 million of these, and each received about one third of an acre. This division did little to increase agricultural production. The skip followed naturally, beginning in 1953 with cooperative farming. Resources were pooled, and, though farmers nominally still owned their land, it was in effect worked in common. By 1958, they were ready for the final jump, the ideal, the people's communes. These were to be involuntary units of up to five thousand families, living and working together in collective agricultural projects and small industrial enterprises.

The first commune was opened at Chengtu and called Sputnik. It was much larger than any cooperative, and it incorporated not only agriculture, but industry, education, public health, all social and most domestic functions, which were removed from individual or family control. It also offered no material incentives, and was unwieldy. The peasants were confused and demoralized. The weather turned bad. Dams, too hastily built, collapsed, and as a result of a campaign to eliminate sparrows, the crops were overrun by insect pests. The result was chaos, and the communes began breaking down into smaller village units.

Industry shared with agriculture in the great leap and took the same tumble. Initially, the Communists had made no intrusion on private domestic industry. What there was of it was vital to the postwar economy. Then, gradually, private enterprise began to feel the pressure that had eliminated foreign business. From private business to joint private-state management, the economy was nationalized. In general, as with Communist experience everywhere, nationalization of industry showed good results. While before World War I there wasn't a plant for manufacturing bicycles in China, they were now making 12,000-kilowatt steam turbines and jet planes.

The Great Leap, when it came, showed immediate paper success. Statistics may have been inflated, for gradually transportation snarled, materials ran out, products grew shoddy to keep up the quota, and workers were exhausted, thanks to long hours and the food shortages. By 1962, the Great Leap was over in all but name, and Canada and Australia were putting food on Chinese tables.

Mao next set out to improve his people's minds. Probably he was worried that the leap had left many with a sense of disillusionment. In any event, he announced a cultural and spiritual revolution. It was not his first campaign for mental uplift. In 1949, he had instituted a program at the college level to reform intellectual thought through social and political reeducation and purification. This operation had involved group discussions, confession, and self-criticism; then, finally, submission and, hopefully, a rebirth. Those who did not fully experience the process knew enough to keep their mouths closed. In fact, by 1957, artists and playwrights seemed to Mao well enough reeducated to put an end to censorship. He publicly announced, "Let One Hundred Schools of Thought Contend, and One Hundred Flowers Bloom." Criticism of the regime was instant, vituperative, and upsetting to Chairman Mao. Not flowers, but stinkweeds had blossomed, to his way of thinking, and within the year a new movement, the "Dedication of Hearts Campaign," was under way. This implied that intellectuals had better surrender their hearts to the party or shut up.

The Cultural Revolution   But the Cultural Revolution initiated in 1966 came at a time of more broadly based discontent. The Great Leap had failed. Relations with Russia were bad, and they had soured with several hitherto promising African countries. An iron broom was needed to sweep the stable clean and make a new spiritual start. That broom was the Red Guard, named for the Russian factory workers who in 1905 bled for the revolution. In China, of course, they were not factory workers, but students, from fifteen years of age up to the early twenties. They were only too happy to close down the universities and take off on "Long

Marches" to save the revolution. *The Quotations* of Mao was in every knapsack.

To kick matters off, Mao himself was shown swimming down the Yangtze River, nine miles in sixty-five minutes, an Olympic record. With such an example, the Red Guards ran wild. Their goal was to perfect the human personality and purge it of noncommunist and foreign poisons. Up went xenophobic wall posters denouncing all who opposed Mao's thought. An end was put to the sale of luxury goods, perfumes, cosmetics, all that might appeal to degenerate neocapitalists. The names of streets and shops incompatible with Mao's thinking were changed. Revisionists were given dunce caps to wear, and they were made to sit on stools while the "revolutionary masses" taunted them and occasionally trampled them to jelly. Ideally, exploitation was being swept away to leave room for devotion to socialist public interest, but very quickly all control was lost and with it all purpose.

The whole reason for choosing the Red Guards for the mission was their subservience to the party rather than to the army, which Mao distrusted. Now he needed the army to limit the hysteria, which went so far as to invade the sanctity of a Soviet merchant ship in the port of Dairen, humiliate its captain, and provoke a dangerous international incident. There were armed clashes in the streets and untold casualties; there were even rumors of civil war in China. Then, gradually, the turbulence subsided. Schools reopened with some reluctance on the part of staff and students, but by this time the party apparatus was in shambles and the army, while carrying Mao through the crisis, had grown to ominous stature.

The fiasco of the Cultural Revolution must have come as a sobering slap in the face for all concerned. For the radical Red Guards the outcome was more than a mere slap. It meant jail or a firing squad or flight to Hong Kong. Now farmers are more regularly working their own private plots, and, in the provinces, soldiers have replaced the police. What some would call bureaucratic revision and others pragmatic conservativism has moved to the fore in China. That communism, the party, and Mao survived the disaster of the Cultural Revolution at all is owing to a generally strong nationalism and the widespread realization that, despite occasional blind-staggers, communism has done much for China. It has achieved the political unification of a vast and diverse land. It has stamped out banditry, warlordism, and exploitation by foreign powers, as well as much disease and starvation. Under communism, China at last stands up in the modern world, and she casts a mighty shadow. As has been said, "Once everything changed except China; now, in China, all changes." This is recognized with pride by the average Chinese, who did not go uninformed in 1970 when the government orbited its first small satellite, happily broadcasting the singsong tune: "Dong Fang Hong"—"The East Is Red." Domestically, communism has done well by the average Chinese citizen. A plateau of sufficiency from which some other form of government would more usefully lead is still far in the future.

The Present Day The Cultural Revolution did much to alter China's international stance as well. As long as it raged, China existed in a partial quarantine. She has returned to the international scene, apparently chastened. True, the Sino-Soviet split survived the Cultural Revolution intact. Thirty-five Russian divisions still crowd the northern frontier, and, in 1969, fighting erupted at Chen-Pao Island on the Ussuri River. However, diplomatic efforts are being made toward settlement. Otherwise, China is working hard for new friendships and is courting foreign visitors from both East and West. A particular effort has been made in the Afro-Asian area, an effort no longer as directly keyed to the revolution. Whether the fruits of Peking's diplomacy will be sweet or sour cannot yet be ascertained. Behind the euphoria surrounding the Chinese and American rapprochement, there are many real problems. There are the obvious questions of Taiwan, the role China will play in the United Nations, the shifting of international relationships involving particularly the Soviet Union and Japan, the future alignment of Southeast Asia. Until his death in 1976, Premier Chou En-lai was the center of all these negotiations. Unlike Party Chairman Mao, Chou was not peasant-born, but descended from the mandarin, or ruling class. He was world-traveled, spoke English, and was a formidable negotiator who thrived on complex problems. Hua Kuo-feng, who was chosen to replace him, still remains an enigma to most of the Western world, and the present unrest in China is an equally unknown quantity in relation to international diplomacy.

Dogmatic communism in Red China is undoubtedly not out of gas, but it is clearly, for the moment, suffering engine trouble. This is probably a good thing for the world, though in the long run, if serious trouble comes from China, it is as likely to come from over-population as it is from Communist doctrine. China is a giant, the very creature of its own ancient mythology that held that the earth was carved out by a Titan who, at his death, became the elements: his flesh the soil, his blood the rivers and oceans. The race of humans were the parasites feeding on his remains. There may be a limit to such a corpse, but seemingly none to the Chinese people who increase at the rate of 15 million a year and will very soon reach a total of 1 billion. The question is: How long can Mao's stumbling leaps forward keep ahead of the alternatives to expand or starve?

The Third World
and Communism

Caught between the dark past and the cybernetic future, between colonialism and independence, between the pressures of capitalism and communism, are many individual nations in large areas of the globe sometimes grouped together and called the Third World. These emergent nations are found in the Arabic Middle East, in black Africa, and in Southeast Asia, and considering these areas together is justified on the basis of certain elemental factors that are common to all of them. All of these areas were formerly largely controlled by white Western capitalism. In the space of half a century, not only has that control been removed, but the invincible image of the white Westerner has been shattered by two world wars. There is now high motivation among the people of these areas to make good on their own merits, an objective made difficult by massive poverty, endemic disease, and want of education. Sometimes helping, often hindering, and always confusing these nations in their efforts at self-improvement is the competition between ideologies—capitalism, socialism, and communism—all striving to show the way into the future. Communist assertions have naturally been received diversely by each and every country in this Third World, and, for the sake of an orderly discussion, it must be separated into the areas mentioned above.

The Middle East   In the Arabic Middle East, the ancient lands stretching from Morocco to Iraq, a common religious heritage exists. Though the conquests of Islam at one time encompassed a vast empire, there has been much decay, colonizing, and breaking away. Islam, though still a strongly shared experience, is no longer the binding force that it was. Today there are twenty Arab nations: democracies, monarchies, Socialist republics, and tyrannies. What does bind together this mass of humanity, with its kings, princes, presidents, and dictators, is a common language: Arabic. More than a language, Arabic is a way of thinking, and this is what one has in mind when one speaks of the Arab mentality and the Arab world. World War II and its consequences ushered in another binding element, the creation of Israel on Arab soil. To the Arabs, Israel's claim to the Holy Land is no more legitimate than was the claim of the Italians when they invaded Libya and put spotlights on the statues of the Caesars. Both are expressions of colonialism under which Egypt and much of the Arab world labored for centuries.

Domestically, communism has had hard going in the area. Its early pre-World War II cells attracted primarily members of the foreign minorities: Jews, Greeks, French. Many of these Communists have been thrown out of the Arab countries, while communism at the Arabic grass roots has been a failure. It is looked upon as a foreign and godless import for which the average Arab has no use and no frame of reference. Sometimes, for the sake of favors from Russia, local parties have been tolerated as long as they undertook no revolutionary activities. Yet from Marrakesh to Baghdad, jails are crowded with Arab Communists.

Typical was the recent suppression in Sudan, where the Arab world's largest Communist party was broken up in the summer of 1971, and the leaders, including a

Lenin Peace Prize winner, were executed. Despite this violence and the evidence that Soviet military advisers were involved in the domestic subversion, Russian MIG fighters and tanks are too much of a temptation for Sudan to break off relations with Russia. For Russia, Sudan is an important bridge between the Middle East and black Africa, and so, for practical reasons, they too, will undoubtedly swallow their pride.

Egypt The ambivalence shown in Sudan toward communism is typical of the entire Arab world. Included is Egypt, their international spokesman, if the Arabs can be said to have one voice. Egypt has long disavowed communism, and its local adherents, coming mostly from Greek, Jewish, and Armenian minorities, are familiar with Egyptian prison life. Yet Egypt has become increasingly dependent on Soviet aid and advisers and domestically has evolved a system with communisitic overtones.

President Gamal Abdel Nasser christened his new approach Arab socialism, which meant, for him, socialism responsive to the particular needs of the Arabic community and subject to no imported dogma. The economy and everything governmental was in a shambles in 1952 when Nasser supplanted the uninterested playboy King Farouk with his clique of Free Officers. Nasser's evolving system of Arab socialism called for nationalization of the Suez Canal, of banking, and of big industry. There were to be workers' representatives on the board of directors of each company, and each worker was to receive an incentive share of the profits. Retail outlets, artisans, and small enterprises were not controlled. As far as it went, the approach was socialist, the application totalitarian, and the results disappointing.

In the agricultural area, Nasser had grown up with a sincere hatred of the big absentee landowners. They could and did fly in their dinners from Maxim's in Paris while their private armies drove the serfs, the fellahin, out from their fly-infested mud huts to work in the fields. Nasser's love for the oppressed fellahin was personal and sincere, and his measures in their behalf were restrained in the light of such provocations as they suffered. Maximum landholdings were cut at first to two hundred acres, later to one hundred. There was no intention of collectivizing the villagers. In fact, at this lower level, life has remained very democratic and unregimented.

Briefly, then, to contrast Nasser's Arab socialism with communism, it is similar in that its methods at the upper levels are totalitarian and its objectives socialist. In theory, the differences are great. God is acknowledged, and no stateless paradise is anticipated. Private ownership at the lower levels, so long as it is not exploitative, is encouraged, and where assets have been seized by the state, bonds have been given back in compensation to former owners with a ceiling set on income.

What are Egypt's prospects? They seem uncertain at best. The Aswan Dam, in which so much hope was placed, is a questionable success. The population is expanding, and the economy has been drained by military expenditures. The sudden death in 1970 of President Nasser raised another question. Nasser was an Arab Lincoln, risen up from a modest family in a village of the Beni Mor, "The tribe of the bitter," to his height as "Champion of Arabism, Hero of Socialism." A half million throats would proclaim his name as his open car pressed through seething crowds. His successor, Anwar es Sadat is a mild-mannered man with none of Nasser's natural charisma but in terms of measurable achievements he has already surpassed his predecessor, particularly in respect to the 1973 war with Israel. Although not victorious, Egypt was not humiliated on the field, and if the subsequent peace negotiations are honored there is a real hope for future tranquility in the Middle East.

Then, too, Sadat has Russia to contend with. In the

mid-1950s, Egypt needed help. The United States might have given it, but John Foster Dulles' refusal of aid to the Aswan High Dam project, a gap filled by Russia, began a rift that widened irrevocably as the United States extended military aid to Israel. Egypt wanted counterbalancing armaments and received them from Russia. Along with the aid came memories of colonialism, and it was with conflicting thoughts that Sadat, in 1971, purged pro-Soviet plotters from his government while, almost at the same time, he entered a fifteen-year treaty binding Egypt even more closely to the Soviet Union. Egypt and Russia have needed one another. Egypt has wanted arms and defense against Israel. Russia cannot pull out of the area without loss of face throughout the underdeveloped world, and both militarily and politically, the aid has strengthened the Soviet position in the Mediterranean area. However, the October war of 1973 against Israel, though tending to prove the merit of Soviet arms, has actually weakened Russian influence in respect to the United States, which through the subsequent efforts of Secretary of State Henry Kissinger exerted a major influence in the area.

To sum up briefly; domestic communism has very poor prospects throughout the Arab world. As former President Aref of Iraq declared, "Islam alone is absolute justice. We do not need to import principles from abroad." Putting constant power struggles aside, the general alternative drift is toward Arab socialism along totalitarian and military lines. Its chief goal is land reform. This does not imply, as in Russia, the replacement of one class by another, or communization, but ideally a cooperation between private and public sectors with no one being exploited.

Internationally, the emphatic goal of most Arab countries is self-determination. Nonalignment is a cornerstone of policy. Some have called it "Positive Neutrality," which implies a willingness to accept aid, without commitment, from East or West. Soviet Russia

has been favored in recent years as a direct result of
Arab antagonism toward Western-supported Israel.
The division is not inspired by racial or religious preju-
dice. Even the Arabs acknowledge a common heritage
with the Israelis. What scalds and what has turned
Arab countries toward Russia is the conviction that
Israel is the last thorny creature of an old and loathed
tradition of Western imperialism. This specter, which
has haunted the Arab world since Victoria's day, suggests similar Soviet aspirations for the Middle East and
the threat seems now too great to make Russian aid
appealing so long as hopes for a diplomatic settlement
are high.

Africa   To the south, beyond the deserts of North
Africa, are numerous emergent nations, some small, all
militantly separate, but united in terms of the experience of color. This is black Africa, and, in its sometimes strident, boisterous youth, it has been tempted by
a variety of ideologies, not the least influential of which
is communism.

Quite apart from outside pressures, there are local
factors that enhance communism's appeal in the area.
For the black intelligentsia who face a confused future,
the system offers clear-cut techniques for manipulating
society toward a more industrial and, presumably,
more successful future. Then, too, it seems to have an
inherent kinship with the natural communism of the
old tribes, where herds and the fruits of the hunt were
held in common. In a historical perspective, communism repudiates the centuries of exploitation by white
men that are the African's cruel memory: the slave
trade that led to the captivity and death of tens of
millions of black Africans, and more recently, the
Western competition for the natural resources of the
continent.

Factors detrimental to the flowering of communism
in black Africa, however, seem to have greater weight.
There is the "blackness" of Africa, to begin with. Go-

ing beyond the physical reality, it carries a spiritual significance that cannot be shared beyond that continent. It is the basis for the Pan-African movement and for much nationalistic sentiment, and it binds Africans together just as the Arabs are bound by a common tongue. Tribalism, though it has communistic elements, also has democratic ones, such as the practice of giving every man a vote. An inherent tendency to acquiesce in the authority of important chiefs encourages despotism when tribal ways yield to modern statehood. Loyalties shift slowly, from tribe to nation, but already in the more settled and urban areas where leadership first develops, tribalism has largely given way to nationalism.

Colonialism, like tribalism, is a two-edged sword. While the memory of it may leave hostility to Western ideas and control, it does not automatically make communism attractive, for, though Russia and China may protest to the contrary, both have been guilty of imperialism. Like her Arab neighbors to the north, black Africa wants economic help, but no more administration from abroad. Though Hungary and Tibet are more distant than tribal memories of the slave trade, the implications for modern Africa are not discounted. Finally, like the Arabs, black Africans have a strong religious background. Christianity and Islam are less deeply ingrained than their own animism of invisible forces and beings and the spirit world of their ancestors, but all are incompatible with Communist materialism.

Though the dice may be loaded against them there, neither Russia nor China can be accused of not trying to influence Africa. Until recently, these Communist countries had seemed more remote than the moon to the average African, but starting from zero, in the mid-1950s, thousands of their technicians began to arrive in Africa, while hundreds of African students were invited to Russia. This approach certainly did not reflect the thinking of Karl Marx, who had concentrated his future hopes on the industrial society. Africa was beyond his ken; a blank on the map. Lenin was the Communist theorist who first realized the potential of underdeveloped colonial countries. He had rationalized for them a drift from precapitalism straight to communism without the Marxist requisite of a capitalistic period. This prediction was gratifying to all enthusiastic Communists after their early failures in industrial Europe. Nevertheless, during the formative 1920s, Lenin concluded that the proletariat in the colonial countries was too weak to bother with, and his approach would be to support bourgeois democratic forces as a way of gaining influence. It sounded like a practical idea. In operation, however, antifascism became a necessary preoccupation until after 1948, which left Soviet communism little time for African affairs.

Once Communist power in Eastern Europe had been consolidated, however, the Soviets again looked to Africa. In Stalin's view, the world was divided into two irreconcilable camps, the imperialist and the anti-imperialist blocs. He included Russia in the latter despite recent Soviet activity in Eastern Europe and the Balkans. Applying Marxist-Leninist dogma to the colonies in Africa, he decided there would be an inevitable revolt brought on by increasing imperialist oppression from the West. With this in mind, it was the Communist task to prepare the revolutionaries, and the Soviets already had training centers such as the "University of the Eastern Toilers" at Tashkent in the USSR.

The Soviet Union readied itself for a long struggle, only to be taken by surprise. With very little hesitation, most of the Western colonial powers granted the black African states their independence. This ideological disaster for the Communists occurred about the same time as Stalin's denunciation by Khrushchev. Doggedly Moscow began rethinking her policies in the light of the new black African spirit. The national bourgeoisie in these African countries was rehabilitated into a worthy ally, and Russian goals were altered to a long-term political speculation. The hope was to break down fears of the Soviet Union and at the same time to gain influence by force of example. Houses of Soviet Culture were set up. Black students were invited to the Soviet Union for free education and indoctrination. For those who could not go, film vans went out to the villages. They showed how much the Soviet Union loved black people, as well as what work huge Russian-made tractors were capable of doing. In this way, subversion and governmental overthrow gave way to a policy of winning allies in the cold war who, with luck, would become dependent satellites in the long run.

China's approach to the black African scene has been different. Though unable to afford the massive aid doled out by Soviet Russia, she has two advantages. First, her people are not white, a racial factor that has its value, although it is theoretically of no importance in Marxist thinking. Secondly, modern Russia in many ways resembles the former European colonial powers. She is industrialized, while China is still in the process. The African can see things going on in agricultural China that he can immediately apply to his own country.

These similarities and differences in background do not, however, account for the difference in the Chinese and Soviet approaches to Africa, which until recently has been a factor in Sino-Soviet discord. In the Peking view, to support bourgeois Africa, as Russia was doing, was to work against the revolution, a feeling going back to their own experience with Chiang Kai-shek. Consequently, Chinese aid was initially limited to countries susceptible to revolution. Others, including Nasser's Egypt, were denounced and written off as imperialist puppets. China's Premier Chou En-lai toured ten promising African countries in the winter of 1963–1964, and subsequently Radio Peking bombarded them with anti-American, anticolonial messages. Ironically, the speeches were delivered in English. Only recently has the Peking hard line begun to thaw. The trend today seems to be toward promoting allies rather than toward stirring up revolution.

Given the black African setting and the Communist approach, what results have been achieved? To study the rise and fall of essentially self-interested tribal chiefs would lead to endless ramifications. A flavor of the changing scene can be given by briefly considering examples of former Belgian, French, and British colonies, their different preparations for independence, and their reaction to Communist infiltration.

Zaïre   Nowhere was preparation for independence more inadequate than in the Belgian Congo. The Belgian policy provided very limited educational facilities in the Congo, but absolutely no political training for the Congolese in how to run an independent country. As late as 1956, Belgium was blandly discussing the possibility of independence within thirty years. Within two years there was rioting in the Congo, within four a panicked Belgium was pulling out, leaving the huge, tribalized country adrift in the twentieth century, with no established political leaders and exactly twenty-four college graduates. There were numerous aspirants to leadership. Among them was a former postal employee and convicted embezzler, Patrice Lumumba, who escalated the growing confusion first by calling on the United Nations to give aid in what was clearly a tribal dispute and very soon thereafter calling for Russian troops.

The Russians were all too ready to apply their simple class-struggle theories to the complicated cross-currents of tribalism, nationalism, and personal egoism. The tumult increased until General Joseph Mobutu, the head of the army, took over. The Russians were told to depart and they did, leaving the Congo to a more hopeful future. Lumumba was handed over to Katanga tribesmen, who amused themselves by taking him apart slowly: an ear, a nose, a toe, one by one.

President Mobutu Sese Seko has evaded intrigues of

rival leaders and dissident tribes. His prospects are enhanced by a potentially rich economy, and though the Congo, recently renamed the Zaïre Republic, is subject to increasingly repressive measures, it has growing stability. For Soviet Communism, the Congo experience has provided a lesson in staking all on one unstable leader. It has encouraged a more subtle approach to the ex-colonial scene, which by no means fits the simple pattern of Marxist-Leninist doctrine.

Guinea Unlike the paternal Belgian approach, the French wanted to remake their colonials, by their own choice or not, into French citizens. Whenever possible, this meant a French education and some slight introduction to the governmental process. As in the Congo, independence came abruptly to French Guinea in 1958, when Charles de Gaulle put forward a referendum offering French overseas territories the choice of integration with France or complete independence.

Unlike the Congo, Guinea already had a popular hero in Sékou Touré, a member of the old clan known as the "Sword Nobility." His answer to de Gaulle was, "We prefer poverty in liberty to riches in slavery." De Gaulle gave his civil servants sixty days to clear out. "Too slow," thundered Touré, and within eight days the French were gone. But for Touré, chaos would have reigned. He took over in an underdeveloped land of diverse tribal loyalties. His own political theories were neither democratic nor entirely communist. "Communism is not the way for Africa," he said, though he adopted certain Marxist forms. For class warfare, he substituted anticolonial struggle, and he used the heretic cult of the individual as successfully as Hitler or Mao.

Soviet Communism approached this relatively settled state with far more caution than it was to show in invading the Congo. Not arms but a tactful ambassador, Daniel Solod, arrived, and after him came a horde of advisers and technicians. Though the farmers seemed to resent the new collective approach, Russia soon began speaking confidently of the new "people's democracy." As soon as Guinea appeared to have burnt its bridges to the West, however, aid began to dry up. Domestic crises were encouraged to hasten Guinea into the Soviet camp. When promised food arrived from the USSR it was spoiled; grain was already fermenting. Instead of vital tractors came snowplows and toilet seats. Sugar was so treated for humidity that it refused to dissolve in tea.

Despite these problems, the Soviets felt that their plan was working. Procommunist Guineans paraded and rioted in the streets. Once again, however, Russia had jumped the gun. Touré wasn't about to be overturned by a Russian-inspired conspiracy, and in December, 1961, he threw out Ambassador Solod. His objective was not a complete shift to the West, but he knew that Russia was aware that the West would only too happily step in, and he was not overly suprirsed when Anastas Mikoyan hurried to Guinea to smooth things over.

As of 1974 Guinea called itself a one-party republic. Its president Sékou Touré, ruled as a dictator with a police state to support him. Aid came from a cautious if not chastened Soviet Union. Guinea's small army was equipped with Russian helmets and Czech rifles. Refusing to be won over, Touré sacrilegiously described communism as nothing but state capitalism. First and foremost, he is loyal to himself, and then to Africa. What happens next is an open question. The vacuum that will exist after Touré will have to be filled, and it is unlikely to be an easy process.

Ghana Of all the colonial powers in Africa, only Britain acted as though the subjects might eventually become independent. She took the responsibility of training them in self-government. Until 1957, the British Gold Coast basked in the old dream of a bygone kingdom of Ghana ruled over by kings so rich they tethered their horses to gold nuggets. Then part of the dream came true. As the first liberated colony in black Africa, Ghana was reborn, and with this rebirth came a ruler nearly as fabulous as the monarchs of old. This was Kwame Nkrumah, Ghana's first president. He was born in a mud hut and his name means "Saturday's Child." Nkrumha studied at Lincoln University in Pennsylvania and was early impressed by the American Marcus Garvey and his back-to-Africa movement.

Influenced by African tradition, Western education, and the lure of Marxism, Nkrumah described himself as a "Christian, Marxist, Socialist." As president he tended to mix up Marxian theory with the Bible, and for good measure he tied to the arms of his chair of state leather voodoo charms to repel evil spirits. Postcards from Ghana pictured Jesus and Nkrumah hand in hand, but in practice Nkrumah ruled less by messianic love than by fascist police power. Nkrumah's one mistake as a dictator was not to destroy the opposition of tribal chiefs as Touré did in Guinea. A hard core of resistance existed in the Ashanti tribe, and in 1966, while Nkrumah was on his way to visit Peking, the Ashantis rose along with the army, abolished his party, and told him never to return.

Under an army-led National Liberation Council, Lieutenant General Joseph Ankrah took over the government. Ankrah favored friendship with Britain. The British had not been ousted from Ghana in anger as had been the French from Guinea and the Belgians from the Congo. However, faced with accepting Ghanian citizenship or getting out of the country, an alternative colored by Nkrumah's constant harping on the evils of colonialism, many British subjects have departed. Still much private capital remained in the hands of Western businessmen and leading Ghanians have retained a taste for things British; the judges' robes, afternoon tea, cricket on the green, a culture and philosophy retained in form if not entirely in substance. These residual tendencies have been encouraged along with closer Western ties. Under the succeeding Prime Minister, Kofi A. Busia, the trend seemed toward civilian government, British-style socialism, and a balancing of the economy which Nkrumah had left several hundred million dollars in the red.

All this was repudiated in January of 1972 when the Prime Minister was ousted and his cabinet ministers jailed following a military coup led by Colonel Ignatius K. Acheampong. Thus far Acheampong's regime has been a success. His repudiation of the enormous foreign debt and the lowering of certain taxes have made him locally popular in a land which, like a number of emergent nations, seems unprepared to cope with democratic government.

Southeast Asia Southeast Asia lacks the unifying consciousness of blackness found in Africa as well as the pervasive lingual and religious ties that bind the Arab world. Southeast Asia shares with those other areas only the colonial past and the too rapid emergence into an ideologically laden future. Along this line, two simplifications exist. One has been endorsed by United States policy to the effect that there are in Southeast Asia a number of democracy-loving states that, if unprotected, will fall to international communism like a row of dominoes. The other idea derives from Moscow and Peking and pictures an Asiatic people oppressed by the white West, yearning only to bask in the light of the Communist dawn. Existing simultaneously, these notions make for the more or less constant rattle of machine guns.

Despite the lack of homogeneity, a few generalities for political and ideological purposes can be made about Southeast Asia. First, there is the diversity itself. While the anthropologist struggles with ethnic origins, the average Southeast Asian villager is content with the myth that says the human race comes from seeds strewn from a great pumpkin. Skin tone relates to whether a people's seeds emerged from a hole opened with a knife or from one burned through by a red-hot poker. In addition to ethnic dissimilarities, religions are various: Buddhist, Hindu, Islamic, Christian, animist, with many blends and variations. Languages are almost beyond count. There is very little shared history such as one finds in America, and no shared attitudes such as the African "negritude" as described by Léopold Senghor of Senegal. In short, the peoples of Southeast Asia would seem to lack the uniformity of dominoes for Western fears or Communist purposes.

By and large, the average Southeast Asian is nonpolitical. If a farmer is asked where his people originated, he will answer, "Here, in this village." Here his grandparents lived, and that is horizon enough. This average peasant is conservative and loyal to his landlord, king, or tribal chief. Nationalism and dedication to causes is a recent Western innovation with few adherents.

In Southeast Asia, apart from a Western-educated and Western-fattened veneer of politicians and professional people, there is no reason for the average citizen to love or respect the white West. Until World War I, the white colonial seemed invincible and superior. That war reduced his prestige, as did the repercussions of the economic depression that followed. Any lingering respect vanished with the Japanese invasion early in World War II. Then the white colonial was humbled, and there was Japanese talk of Asia for the Asians. This boiled down to a Japanese colonial empire, and, with the war going badly for the Japanese, they proved far harsher masters than the ousted Europeans. They left a bad taste behind them, one that China, as a big, threatening, militant neighbor to the North, has done little to dissipate. China's overrunning of Tibet and its attacks along the Indian border have not helped to distinguish it from Japan. Not that the Asians want the Europeans back, either. What most Southeast Asians long for is simply to be left alone.

That's the last wish the Asians are apt to have fulfilled. If they are lucky, they will have political pressure and massive aid programs, as in the case of India. If they are unlucky, they will have all this plus war, subject to foreign manipulation. Such was the situation in Vietnam and, to a lesser extent, in neighboring Laos and Cambodia.

Vietnam Vietnam, formerly part of French Indochina, has been a battleground for over thirty years. Communism has been a major factor in the struggle from the first, when a native son returned from the Marxist community in Paris and began to burn tax rolls while robbing and killing French officials. This was Ho Chi Minh. The French ruthlessly crushed his insurrections, a process that only heightened among Ho's people his image as a gallant Robin Hood. During the years of Japanese occupation, Ho built up a guerrilla army only to find, with the peace, that he was trapped between the menace of Communist China in the North and the demands of the French at home. Fearing the Chinese more, the Vietnamese allowed the French to remain, subject to future negotiation.

A flood of returning French settlers and troops indicated their adamant intention to stay on forever, and Ho renewed the battle against France and the puppet government under Bao Dai. Ho's fighting doctrine for his Communists was, "You are fish in the water, and the water is the people." The French were outmaneuvered and by 1954 were ready to throw in the sponge. By this time, Ho Chi Minh controlled northern Vietnam and the anticommunist Ngo Dinh Diem held the south with aid from the United States. Diem lasted nine years. In 1963, an assassin finished him, and the long war accelerated again. Now the United States has withdrawn, but the war goes on. Communism has not had a peacetime tryout, and peacetime always proves a harder test for applied ideology than wartime. The one certainty is the strongly nationalistic flavor of Vietnamese communism. China is respected and feared, but she will be allowed control in Vietnam only in extremis.

Laos The issue of communism remains uncertain throughout the rest of Southeast Asia. In some areas its seed has fallen on unreceptive soil. In others it has been violently rooted out. In Laos and Cambodia, the question is more a military than a political matter. Until a few years ago, Laos remained happily isolated, disturbed only by the feudal power-skirmishings of minor princes who spent most of their time banqueting and riding elephants. The people were carefree, isolated, and illiterate, and they were not particularly resentful of their French administration. Then, abruptly, the French pulled out, leaving a natural vacuum for China, Russia, North Vietnam, or the United States to fill and exploit. In June, 1974, the United States withdrew its remaining forces, leaving the final solution undetermined.

Cambodia Cambodia was never a country with Communist leanings. The threat always came from the political whirlpools of neighboring Laos, Vietnam, and Thailand. By 1970, the wars in Vietnam and Laos simply overflowed. The rightist military clique in Cambodia felt obliged to take over from the formerly neutralist Prince Sihanouk, who fled to Peking. Since then the new premier, General Lon Nol, has been resisting North Vietnamese encroachment with increasing aid from the United States. Here again, the solution promises to be military rather than political, and part of the larger picture in the area.

India Southern Asia's largest nation, and one in which Communist infiltration has fortunately taken a milder form than elsewhere, is India. Lenin expected communism to succeed in that country—overcrowded, poor beyond belief—before it did in China. History has frustrated his hopes and hopelessly divided the Communist party in India. The main cause of communism's defeat was the political and religious leader Mahatma Gandhi, who united much of India behind him in his nonviolent drive for independence. Not only was he successful in ousting the British after World War II, he made great strides in dispelling the sense of class and the potential class warfare that is such a primary Communist instrument.

The Communist party of India (CPI) got off to a promising start in the early 1920s, quite oblivious of the endless frustrations to come. Their first mistake, made under Soviet direction, was to oppose Gandhi's movement as bourgeois deception. This position immediately estranged the party from the mainstream of progress. The end of World War II brought the British withdrawal, the success of Gandhi's cause, and his assassination. Left to govern the country was the Congress party, run by Westernized, university-educated Indians. The Communists tried hard to adapt, going so far in the state of Tripana as to campaign for the restoration of the former maharajah—anything to gain popularity.

Real problems for the CPI began with the Sino-Soviet rift. Traditionally the party had Soviet roots, but socially India was better fitted for the Chinese approach. There existed in India no substantial industrial bourgeoisie to be overthrown. While one group in the CPI followed the Russian plan of victory by way of parliamentary means and accepted a general reconciliation with Nehru's socialist policies, the more militant faction advocated overthrow of the government by guerrilla tactics. This "Chinese" minority received a near-death blow in 1962, when China attacked along the Indian frontier. The CPI offices in New Delhi were sacked, and the party rightists called for unity in defense of the Indian motherland. China accused the Indian Communists of national chauvinism, and the pro-Chinese leftist branch of the party set up a parallel party organization, which in 1964 held a separate party congress in Calcutta, while the Russian-oriented majority met in Bombay. The CPI has recovered from the low ebb of those days, but the average Indian still feels no affection for the Chinese behemoth to the North or for the puppet party that carries out its policies in India.

The Future More than any other large area of the world, Southeast Asia lacks the common thread that would provide for a facile summing up. About all that can be said by way of generalization is that a large, uneducated, agrarian mass of diverse humanity has been thrust by recent colonialism into political and ideological turmoil. All of the people are impressed by the power of the United States and China, and they are afraid of both. For many, Russia, though equally awesome, may seem a happy compromise, for it has been the Russian policy there to give aid without strings in hope of wooing the national governments, while the United States and China pull right and left.

It has been the mistake of the United States to see only ill-fitting extremes, Western democracy or Eastern communism, while disregarding thousands of years of religious, racial, and ethnic accord and discord in the area. Even where aid has been sincerely given in the hope of physically benefiting the people, there have been frustrations and setbacks, often caused by the limited Western understanding of Eastern people and their values. Typical is the Laotian village that was a recipient of a massive agricultural aid program. When the village was revisited the following year by officials to see how things were going, the headman explained the abandoned fields by observing, "You showed us how to double our crop last year, so there's no need for us to work this season." In spite of the gap in understanding however, in the long haul there is no other way than by massive aid to dispel the poverty that is the breeding ground for communism.

The best the United States can do for Southeast Asia

and for the rest of the Third World is to give honest assistance where it is needed. At best, living standards can be upgraded. With the elimination of the poverty and ignorance that permit suppression of individuals under totalitarian forms of government, whether of the Right or Left, a freer, more open way of life may be expected. This may seem vague and uninspired counsel for the Western democracies, but there is consolation in the fact that the Communists, with all their concise dogmas, have met with frustrations, too. Typical was the third Afro-Asian solidarity conference held in Tanzania under the very shadow of Mount Kilimanjaro. The hope was to harmonize a Communist front in the Third World. The meeting was a failure. The delegates were in confusion, torn between Russia's talk of coexistence and disarmament and China's endorsement of revolution. On the conference's third day, Kenya's delegate, Oginga Odinga, striving for concert, was driven to proclaim that the Sino-Soviet split was an invention of Western imperialism. Worse was to come. The Indian delegate finally walked out after a dispute with China over Tibet, declaring, "This conference is killed, ruined, finshed; without India there is no conference." No one arose to dispute the point, and perhaps the conclusion applies in general to the situation of communism in the Third World.

Communism in
the Americas

The United States Communism in the United States has had a long but frustrated history. Some of the party's intermediate objectives have been realized over a period of years, although usually through the efforts of noncommunists. The party's primary objective, however, the complete communization of the country, seems less likely now than when the first militant Marxist stepped off an immigrant ship in 1850.

American communism predates even Karl Marx. The ideology's first serious advocate in this country was George Rapp. Like Marx, Rapp was German, and he had read and taken to heart the fourth chapter of Acts: "And the multitude of them that believed were of one heart and one soul: neither said any of them that ought of the things he possessed was his own; but they had all things in common." Convinced of a communistic millennium to come, Rapp moved to the United States in 1803, bringing a congregation with him. This group had given all their property, real and personal, to Rapp and his associates for the benefit of the community, and in return they were guaranteed all the necessities of life. Should they ever desire to withdraw from the group, all their wealth would be returned. Thus was born Harmonie, located in Indiana. The community was augmented later by Robert Owen, an English utopian Socialist who, unlike Rapp, considered religion a superstition. Owen and his more sophisticated group eventually bought out Rapp at the Indiana settlement, for the Germans found the neighborhood attitudes unbearable. Owen renamed the community New Harmony. In the course of time the colony failed, due largely to friction over the theory of equal compensation irrespective of effort or productivity.

Before the demise of New Harmony, Marxist communism had made an enthusiastic if tentative appearance in the United States. Karl Marx himself took much interest in the Civil War, which he saw as a struggle against human bondage. On President Lincoln's reelection, Marx sent him a congratulatory letter that read in part:

> From the very beginning of the titanic American strife, the workers of Europe instinctively felt that the star-spangled banner carried the destiny of their class. . . . The workers of Europe feel sure that, as the American war of Independence initiated a new era of ascendency for the middle class, so the American war against slavery will do it for the working classes.

By this time Joseph Weydemeyer, another Marxist who had arrived in New York with the German immigrant flood of the early 1850s, had found there weren't enough readers for his Marxist magazine, *Die Revolution*. Undiscouraged, he went on to establish the small American Working Men's League, which campaigned against child labor and called for a guaranteed wage. He also sought compulsory education for children too poor to pay for it, as well as state tuition-free colleges. Most of these goals in the course of a century have been realized.

During the 1870s what had been a foreign-born, essentially foreign-speaking, movement began to attract native adherents with startling and party splitting results. Rather stodgy German Marxists found themselves asked to support Victoria Woodhull, an eccentric women's rightist, for President. Her advocacy of free love was for many the last straw.

Marxism and American labor didn't really come to grips until 1890, when Daniel De Leon, a Dutch colonial born in Curaçao, joined the Socialist Labor party in New York. He gained influence in the Knights of Labor just in time to see that powerful labor union fade away, but he remained undaunted. The year 1902 brought inspiration with the Pennsylvania coal strike. For the first time, organized labor successfully blocked a strategic industry for months without being condemned as a revolutionary menace. De Leon sensed the time was ripe for new radical leadership, and in 1905 he succeeded in taking over a newly formed Chicago labor organization. Made up of many anti-AFL groups, this revolutionary group called itself the Industrial Workers of the World. In time it became known as the IWW or "Wobblies." De Leon's efforts, however, to convert it to Marxism failed, and he was ousted.

De Leon was the last of the serious pre-Russian revolutionary Socialists. When the American Communist party was founded in 1919, it was Russian-oriented. The German and American radical past was completely forgotten. Out of the night of the First World War a new day was dawning, and the brightness came only from the East. It was a stormy day, full of strikes and labor unrest. In fact, the war had strengthened American capitalism, and the unrest was less a stirring of an attempt to overthrow the system than a revelation of a desire on labor's part to squeeze out more benefits for themselves. Still, the Communists were largely blamed, and the government-sanctioned crackdown drove the two branches of the party, one mostly foreign-born and Russian-oriented, the other native-born and more naturally democratic, into the underground. This outlawing of the party made it easier for American Communists to identify with Russian Bolshevism, and the native elements were absorbed into the Comintern.

However loudly the Comintern professed equality between national parties, the Soviet Union was predominant from the start. With the rise of Stalin, communism everywhere became subservient to the dictates of Russia. This has been a heavy cross, which the American party has borne with difficulty throughout its existence.

Stalin's hard-left revolutionary turn at the Sixth World Congress in 1928, a move responsive solely to Russia's internal affairs, left the American party floundering, a state from which it was rescued by the economic depression and Hitler's rise to power. The dreary combination suggested the decay of capitalism and seemed to hold out communism as a new faith for all mèn. Workers and unemployed housewives increased the party ranks in the early thirties, although the movement remained a weak one. At the Seventh World Congress, the Comintern about-faced and took up the United Front of democracy against fascism. Party membership reached one hundred thousand. From the denunciation of bogus American democracy, the party switched to a new slogan, "Through Democracy to Socialism." American Communists became obsessed with the civil war in Spain. Many were recruited into that struggle, and many, it was said, learned to die before they learned to fight. These were the pure, heroic idealists. They would not appear again as lifeblood for the American Communist party.

That fascism prevailed in Spain was only the first of countless disillusioning shocks to come. Mother Russia's cynical military pact with Nazi Germany in 1939 left the American party limp and confused. Justifying the pact as a consequence of French and British treachery was more than most American Communists could swallow. Nor did glossing it over help, as Molotov did when he remarked to Ribbentrop, "Ideology is only a matter of taste." Still, the hard core rallied, called for labor strikes against American mobilization, and shouted, "The Yanks aren't coming." Right up until June 21, 1941, American Communists were busily organizing a National Peace Week. The next day, Germany invaded Russia. Peace Week died, to be replaced by American People's Mobilization Week. The pressure to strike was immediately replaced by a demand for an eighty-hour work week. Such opportunism left a bad taste behind it that to some extent evaporated after Pearl Harbor. Before the war ended, "Meadowlands" as sung by the Red Army Chorus had made the hit parade, and the darkly sinister Stalin had become just plain "Uncle Joe," who marched shoulder to shoulder with Uncle Sam.

Under the wartime leadership of Earl Browder, most American Communists came to imagine this bond between the United States and the USSR would be a permanent one. It was not to be. Once the war ended, the world promptly divided: the Free versus the Slave world, in American terminology; imperialist warmongers versus peace-loving Communists, if one preferred Soviet verbiage. Earl Browder, who had given the party an American image during the war, was branded a revisionist and cast out. William Foster, an old hard-liner who favored the class struggle, took his place.

Difficult days lay ahead. In the early 1950s, the intensifying cold war led to a host of communist trials in the United States. Conviction no longer depended on an actual attempt to overthrow the government, but simply upon whether Communists had agreed (that is, conspired) to teach the overthrow of the government. This crime, which was defined by the Smith Act in 1941, was twice removed from actual violence. Under such pressure the party members, relying on the motto "Better fewer, but better," contracted to a hard core and went underground again. The storm raged above them and was spread by Senator Joseph McCarthy's investigations far beyond the bounds of communism. University professors, trade unionists, Jews, atheists, liberals, Socialists, and "nonconformists" in general were attacked. In an atmosphere of fear and repression the testimony of such former Communists as Whitaker Chambers was used against officials like Alger Hiss. The conviction of the Rosenbergs of wartime conspiracy to spy for Russia led to their execution. McCarthy described his effort as "the fight for America." The fruits of these investigations, so far as finding an anti-government plot, were nil. No more evidence was turned up than the FBI already had in its files. With the return to sanity, there were those in Washington who thought that McCarthy's disruption and degradation of American government had temporarily achieved results that went beyond Communist hopes.

Though American communism had weathered the federal trials and had scarcely been touched by McCarthy's inquiries, a near-mortal blow was soon to follow. It came from within, at a time when convicted party members were being freed from jail and the party was returning to the surface. Cold-war antagonisms were easing. The American Communist party seemed on the verge of a second springtime when Stalin was denounced. He had been the oracle and the refuge in every calamity, the source of blind faith in moments of despair. The crisis was far more profound in the United States than in Europe, where the movement was a functioning part of the working class. In the United States, the party drew its strength primarily from idealists and intellectuals who now saw their convictions blown away.

By 1957, three factions attended the Communists' national party convention. William Foster's far-left Stalinist group was doomed from the start. On the other hand, a group clustered behind John Gates, publisher of the *Daily Worker*, the Communist party paper. These, generally, were New York intellectuals who wanted the right to think for themselves now that the old dogmas were discarded. It was the same feeling that led to revolt in Poland and Hungary. It was equally unsuccessful and caused massive resignation and a weakening of the party from which it has never recovered.

Only the middle-of-the-roaders, behind Eugene Dennis, survived. Today the party is reduced in membership to some ten thousand. It continues under the leadership of Gus Hall, its Minnesota-born general secretary. Once again it is almost respectable. With headquarters at 23 West Twenty-sixth Street in New York, it publishes the *Daily World* and suffers from the most damning realization in its history: it has become old-fashioned.

The labor movement has simply passed it by. Unions needed no advice from Moscow. They have their own muscle. So has the American Negro. Back in 1925, the black seemed the best Communist bet in the United States, and an "American Negro Labour Congress" was established. In 1932 a Negro, James Ford, ran for vice-president on the Communist ticket. Most of his votes came from whites. The majority of blacks called him "Red Uncle Tom," and in this label lies the key to Communist failure with this group. Like the African of today, the American black doesn't want to be used. He has his own organizations, from the moderate NAACP to the radical Black Panthers. This growing militancy on the part of younger blacks has raised Communist hopes. It was with a war whoop of joy that the American party leapt to the legal defense of Angela Davis, a glamorous black teacher and professed Communist, who was accused of supplying weapons that were subsequently used to commit murder. But even these melodramatics can attract few blacks who, on the average, are "bourgeois" at heart. They want what the white man already has, property and economic power.

A more recent and seemingly fertile field for recruitment in the United States has been the college campus. There, the Communist activity of the new intellec-

tual Left has centered in the Students for a Democratic
Society. The hope is to move students' views from
liberal to anticapitalist, from reform to revolution, but
there are difficulties. The SDS adopted not only the
red Communist flag but the black of anarchism and
nihilism, offering no replacement for the existing order.
Traditionally, Marxists and anarchists are bitter enemies, and what communism desires is controlled revolution, not guerrilla warfare. Now even the SDS is
becoming leg-weary and old hat. Its numbers have declined sharply, and American communism is left groping for somewhere to go.

Latin America   More than any other continent con-
taining several independent states, Latin America
shares a common heritage. It was colonized by Portu-
gal and Spain, Latin countries of similar culture. Theirs
are the two principal languages spoken, and there is
one Catholic religion throughout. Popular revolution
during the nineteenth century achieved independence
from Europe but generally left in control a European-
ized aristocracy that held the land with military support. The mass of peasants—native Indians, ex-African
slaves and mixed bloods—lived in semiservitude.

This opposition of rich versus poor with the catalyst
of an emerging intelligentsia seemed, after World War
I, to offer a tempting Communist target. Marx had
shown no interest in South America, even though his
son-in-law, Paul Lafargue, had been born in Cuba. The
first radical ideas were introduced by immigrant workers in the mid-nineteenth century. There were more anarchists than Marxists among them. Official communism arrived only after the First World War; in 1918
in Argentina, three years later in Chile, and four
years after that in Cuba. These organizations were
small, dissent-riven, and quite unable to keep abreast
of upheavals within Russia. The confusion drove party
leader Luis Emilio Recabarren to suicide in Chile,
while in Cuba the party's founder, Julio Antonio

Mella, was assassinated. Only since the Second World War has communism in Latin America borne anything but bitter fruit.

Mexico   Unlike the Communist party in the United States, the party in Mexico has generally been allowed to operate in the open without stigma. The fact is that there are, to the detriment of communism in general, two competitive parties: the original Mexican Communist party and the People's party of 1948, which operates now under the name Partido Popular Socialista, and which absorbed the very small Mexican Worker-Peasant party in 1963. In terms of practical results, the Mexican Communists have shared in the United States failure, but for different reasons.

The principal cause for their lack of success was timing. The Communists came too late. Mexico had already endured its bloody revolution, which began in 1910. The emerging government has its ear to the ground for malcontents, it gives concessions, removes unpopular governors, and adjusts wages before trouble can get out of hand. This alertness, coupled with general faith in the good life to come from the established Mexican system, provides barren ground for subversion. This is not to say that the Communist party has failed to make a sincere effort since its establishment in 1919. Its founder was an Indian nationalist, Manabendra Nath Roy, who had studied at Stanford University. He got into trouble and from trouble into jail. From there, he fled to Mexico.

Initially, efforts were made to influence organized labor, without success. The Mexican peasants were isolated, unpolitical, and hard to recruit. In the end, party control fell entirely to intellectuals and particuarly to artists. Diego Rivera, David Alfaro Sigueiros, and José Orozco are all famous painters, and their support has given Mexican communism publicity beyond its actual strength.

Political power in Mexico since 1929 has rested in

the official government party, called since 1946 the Institutional Revolutionary party. Under President General Lázaro Cárdenas in the late thirties, social, economic, and educational reforms were undertaken. Gradually the army was eased out of politics, while the government bureaucracy has grown enormously. The business community has enlarged its political influence, changing the revolution's original goal of dividing up the economic cake into one of making the cake bigger.

The army as a creation of the revolution has never objected to nonmilitary tasks, such as dealing with unruly students or with restless political parties should they show signs of operating outside the accepted political framework. Other factors standing in the way of Communist growth in Mexico are the strong Catholic Church and a culture that is basically Western in attitude. The great revolutionary hero Benito Juárez, though a full-blooded Zapotec Indian, succeeded less because of his blood than because he was a lawyer and statesman educated in the Western tradition. Nor is the anticolonial argument as persuasive as it is in Africa or the Arab world, for Mexico threw off all Spanish and French connections over a hundred years ago. Although the United States may at times be feared or envied, Mexico's political problems for the last several generations have been her own, and thus far she has provided adequate solutions.

In fact, the government is now so stable that the Communists in Mexico have been given wide freedoms, encouraged, perhaps, by Mexico's own revolutionary memories, which show a blend of liberalism and socialism. So long as any party "plays the game," there is no trouble. This means accepting the government, with criticisms limited to specific persons and actions, refraining from interference in foreign policy, and making no links with foreign governments. To overstep these limits is an invitation to the police and the army. Otherwise, the Communists are free to publish and free to use Mexico as a political haven, as many United

States Communists did during the conspiracy trials of the 1950s—as Trotsky had done before them. At present, Mexico is economically healthy, and the Institutional Revolutionary party shows no signs of losing dominance. Unless there are drastic changes, the Communists within the country will have nothing tempting to offer.

Cuba Communism's most spectacular victory in Latin America has come in Cuba, which, in point of fact, was more inheritance than victory. The leader in the revolt was Fidel Castro. Born in 1927 in Oriente Province, Castro was educated in Santiago and Havana and received his law degree at Havana University in 1950. Three years later, his attack on the military barracks in Santiago de Cuba touched off a resistance of disgruntled, land-hungry peasant farmers against the dictator Batista, who was supported by the big estate owners. By 1958, this old regime was on the run. Robin Hood had bested the Sheriff of Nottingham, and most Americans applauded. Cuban as well as international Communists had been taken by surprise. They were of the older urban industrial school of Russian Communists. Castro and his followers, though they may not have realized it at the time, had followed more closely the Chinese pattern of revolution.

The official Communist party of Cuba had gotten off to an early start in 1925. Russia gave the directives, but the impressive resistance of the Chinese Communist Army against the Kuomintang did not go unnoticed. The political opponents chosen by the Cuban Communists were not the establishment, but those parties which competed for dominance of the political Left; reformers, anarchists, Trotskyites. These might steal Communist fire, while, hopefully, the establishment would provide a ripe and useful target for orthodox Communist revolution. With this in mind, Fulgencio Batista was supported enthusiastically in his rise to dictatorial power. The orthodox Communists were right to the extent that Batista created excellent cause for a revolution, but by the time Castro had decided that Russia was a more desirable ally than the United States, the old Cuban Communist party was out of a job. Batista fled the country January 1, 1959. Many refugees were to follow him. These unhappy exiles, concentrated in Florida, attempted an invasion of Cuba with surreptitious aid from the United States. This 1961 fiasco was firmly put down by the Cubans at the Bay of Pigs.

Fidel Castro is no theoretical communist. He has shown scorn for philosophers who tend to overlook practical problems, particularly since the removal of the militant Che Guevara from the Cuban scene. Many of Castro's pragmatic programs have shown positive results. A vigorous campaign to enlist "people's teachers" was instituted under the slogan "The people will teach the people." This program has done much to enhance the quantity if not the quality of education. Lessons for the illiterate, two hours a day after working hours, begin with a fifteen-lesson primer entitled *Venceremos* ("We shall conquer"). Once the student can read this book and can write a letter to Fidel saying so, he will move on ideally to more advanced work.

The Cuban Revolution was dedicated to far-reaching reforms, and the rest of Latin America has shown an inclination to try the same path. In Cuba United States property was seized, and all large private enterprises were nationalized in the usual manner. Landholdings were cut to a maximum of 1,000 acres with the surplus going to renters, sharecroppers, and peasants. Later, the maximum private acreage was cut to 167 acres. Still, individual farmers managed to survive and to hold 45 percent of the land, selling their produce on the free market at a price above the official prices. The state needs these farmers' support, for their farms operate more efficiently than the state-run farms which at present cannot alone meet the demands.

The problem with the latter is incentive. The Cuban

peasant is used to being driven mercilessly. Formerly, the impetus was fear of starvation. That fear has now been removed, but positive incentives are few. As yet, no physical coercion has been applied, but the voluntary mobilization of the youth into semimilitary work forces is proving far from a successful answer, particularly when the national fervor that at first accompanies popular revolution is bound to be on the wane. For the time being, however, such mobilization remains a useful device. It has been particularly successful on the Isle of Pines, rechristened the Isle of Youth, where thousands of young people live collectively, working on the state citrus groves.

Meanwhile, the independent farmer subsists. Since the state still needs him, there is no threat of his farm being taken by fiat. However, over the long haul the regime has devised a policy of attrition to eliminate him. Though his son may inherit his farm, his land may not be sold, and where there is no heir, the state confiscates the property. Other restrictive regulations kept farmers from a wholesale market by a limitation on the purchase in the free market to twenty-four pounds in bulk. Motorized private transportation has virtually disappeared, which inhibits marketing. The upgrading of produce in state stores is expected, and this will contribute to the elimination of demands on the free market.

Private ownership outside of agriculture has been drastically curtailed. While major industries were immediately appropriated by the state, small private enterprises such as bars and food shops resisted until 1968. Then over 57,000 small businesses were nationalized, and their former owners were screened for other employment, usually agricultural. Left out of this mass appropriation were only the owners of private trucks and cabs, whose businesses cannot outlast the life of their fast-deteriorating equipment. The main reason for this drastic step of nationalization, of course, was to put an end to the demoralizing effect of private enterprises on a public otherwise dependent on the state.

Postrevolution Cuba was slow to assert itself in foreign affairs. It wasn't until 1961 that Castro announced his conversion to Marxism-Leninism. A few months later, with his second Havana Declaration, he set forth a blueprint for the exportation of the Cuban system to the rest of Latin America, a kind of Latin American Communist Manifesto that called for revolution first and then communism to follow. This doctrine failed to recognize that, despite anti-Yankeeism in South America, that continent has many strong Western cultural links. Latin American Communists may speak of the "glorious Cuban Revolution," but they still reject Castro's bloody methods and resent his criticisms. Most South American Communists, being also nationalists, do not want the help of agents outside their countries and have informed Castro that he is not "the pope of Revolution."

In the autumn of 1962, the construction of Soviet missile bases in Cuba led to another dangerous confrontation, this time between Russian supply ships and American naval vessels. Fortunately, the Russians agreed to remove the rocket launchers, and the crisis passed. The result was a humiliation for Premier Khrushchev and the warming of Cuban–Red Chinese relations, an additional affront to the Soviet Union.

Red China, along with Che Guevara, remained prominent in Cuban politics during Castro's active campaign to export violent revolution to South America. Che Guevara was the romantic personification of insurrection, and a bit too much for Castro himself to handle. Guevara's departure to South America must have brought a sigh of relief to many Cubans, and his death there, while loudly lamented, surely caused that sigh to be repeated. Like Guevara, Red China held brief sway in Cuba. As the clamor for revolution subsided, the Maoists were accused of trying to strangle the Cuban economy while at the same time subverting the army. Reliance shifted back to Russia. Her technicians have been sent to Cuba and industrial aid will be forthcoming as long as Castro makes his foreign policy statements in muted tones. Cuban support for the invasion of Czechoslovakia in 1968 was gratifying to the Soviets, and the evident success of Russia's policy of cooperation with the more moderate Left in Chile has done much to restore Castro to the Soviet camp.

Prospects for Cuba are mixed. Politically, the island is stable, largely owing to Castro's personality. He is still beloved and revered. Economically, however, progress has been disappointing. Diet remains austere, clothing scarce, new housing almost nonexistent, despite large Soviet investments in oil, electric power, farm equipment, and industrial automation. While the people are used to a paternalistic government, the wild enthusiasm that got the revolution off to a good start has already begun to lag. Cuban communism set impossible goals for itself. They have not been attained, and the dream of nirvana fades. The threat from without, which has sustained many an embattled country, has also disappeared. Invasion from the United States is no longer expected. The Cuban Revolution has passed its emotional peak, and the new threat of decay from within is being met in the usual totalitarian form. The communistic party bureaucracy has begun to harden. Artistic and literary freedom is being cut back, and there is rigid insistence on the official view. The recent government move against poet Heberto Padillo is a case in point. As long as Castro remains strong, his programs will be followed, however limpingly. What will happen if he weakens is beyond prediction.

Chile　The only other Latin American country to experiment with a Socialist Marxist government was Chile. Theoretically, unlike other Communist countries, political changeover was achieved by democratic election, without benefit of outside interference or subversion. Since the days of her own revolution, Chile has been fiercely independent. A typical story reflecting the spirit of the people is that of a captain in the rebel cause whose shattered arm had just been amputated. He returned to the fray with the severed limb held on high, shouting, "Viva La Patria!"

For almost three hundred quiet years, the country was a minor province under Spanish control. The drive for independence began in Chile during the Napoleonic Wars. The country's first ruler, Bernardo O'Higgins, was committed to the ideals of representative government and democracy. To this end, he forbade the use of titles and coats of arms, and he tried to foster a small farmer class at the expense of the *mayorazgos*, the large landholders. Here he was in trouble, for the aristocracy joined with the conservative clergy and forced O'Higgins to abdicate. By 1833, the landed interests had won out, and the right to vote was limited to the literate and well-to-do. This set the pattern of restricted prosperity that is behind Chile's present upheavals.

Throughout the following century, the government remained stable. Reforms were slowly adopted and there developed in the people a great respect for law and order, and an expectation of social reforms within the governmental structure. Indicative of this unique orderliness in Chile are the sidewalk vendors of the latest laws. Their cry is, "A law for today, Señor," and the citizens buy the printed copies with avid interest.

During the 1920s, a Communist party developed in Chile and received much support of an intellectual nature. In 1948, at a time when Russia was first becoming interested in Latin America, the party was briefly declared illegal. For a time, particularly during John Kennedy's Alliance for Progress program, the Communists seemed to lose ground. More popular was the newly emergent Christian Democratic party, which called for "revolution with freedom."

Unfortunately, Chile's economic crisis is almost beyond political solution. Her national economy has always depended upon one major export. Until the end of World War I, it was nitrates, with the business largely in British hands. Subsequently, it has been copper, with the United States taking charge. The decline of one cent per pound in the price of copper in the world market means that Chile loses $15,000,000 in annual revenue. Such helpless dependency on foreign business interests produced agitation for the nationalization of industry long before the Communists took over the government. Then Chile began to nationalize the copper mines owned by Anaconda and Kennecott, without repayment. A low profit margin brought continued economic crisis.

While the national economy of Chile is dominated by foreign interests, land ownership has long been concentrated in the hands of a small Chilean elite. The work is done by tenant farmers feudally dependent on their patron for food, clothing, and protection. This economic stranglehold began to break up with the enlargement of the working middle classes. They banded together against the political tyranny of the aristocracy in 1920, and their Liberal Alliance candidate, Arturo Alessandri, was elected president. He achieved much reform legislation, but it was insufficient to keep pace with mounting social and economic problems. The rich landowners still controlled 86 percent of the arable land, and the rural population of Chile, about one third of the total population, remained poverty-ridden. Urban workers fared little better, for wages have never kept up with the fearful inflation. From 1940 to 1950 prices rose over 400 percent, and from 1950 to 1960, over 2000 percent. Even public servants often subsist on one meal a day, and the consequence of such impossible inflation has been to attract not only the working but the middle class to the far left.

By 1958, the Alliance party, led by Alessandri's son, Jorge Alessandri Rodriguez, barely won by 30,000 votes over a Marxist-backed Socialist-Communist coalition, and, six years later, his party was not even in the race. Opposing the extreme left was Eduardo Frei, a

Christian Democrat, whose program was scarcely less radical than that of the Communists. Frei won, and proposed a "revolution with freedom." The goal was to be one of raising the country's material condition, not in the paternalistic manner, but in such a way as to promote human values. Fine words, but difficult of achievement. A large population increase was causing an urban drift. Shantytowns—autonomous communist villages, self-governed, and aggressively independent— were everywhere. Industrialization was needed to broaden the economic base, but about 25 percent of the citizens lived at a bare subsistence level and there was no market in the country for manufactured goods.

During his term of office, Frei successfully increased copper production, but all the while his Christian Democrats were under challenge from the Right and Left. It was more like a workers' strike than a rebellion when some of the Chilean Army mutinied in 1969 for more pay. Though the economy was growing, so were problems, and Frei's one six-year term was running out. He could not succeed himself, and the Christian Democrats could offer no satisfactory successor. On the other hand, the Communist-Socialist alliance put forward Salvador Allende Gossens, a fiery Socialist-Marxist, and the neat formula of Marxism seemed to offer a plan, an ideology, and the plausible answer to all problems. The Christian Democratic vote was nibbled away by a rightist law-and-order party led by former president Jorge Alessandri Rodriquez. Allende came out the winner in September, 1970, with 36 percent of the votes cast.

Allende was an avowed Marxist, but not a Communist in the traditional sense. For one thing, he disclaimed the necessity of revolution to bring about social change. However, the Communist party of Chile was one of the major groups in his Popular Unity coalition party. New agrarian reform laws limited individual holdings in Chile to 176 acres of irrigated land or 600 of nonirrigated pasture. Where change moved too slowly, peasants seized estates illegally, but most Chileans retained respect for law and order. Simon Bolívar, hero of South American liberation, held out hopes for Chile when he said, "If any republic is to last a long time in America, I think it will be that of Chile. . . . Chile can be free."

It was not for Allende to fulfill this prediction. On September 11, 1973, following a period of paralyzing strikes, economic chaos, cabinet crisis, and street brawling a military junta led by General Augusto Pinochet Ugarte demanded the president's resignation. Allende, by radio broadcast, refused. The air force strafed his palace, took it by assault, and found Allende dead, as was his dream of democratic Marxist-Socialism. Subsequently the military leaders formed a fifteen-member cabinet with Ugarte as the president. They vowed to "exterminate Marxism" throughout Chile and to expel the allegedly more than ten thousand foreign "extremists" to whom Allende had given refuge. Thousands were arrested, many were summarily executed. Relations with Cuba were cut while foreign investment in mining was again encouraged. Today one more South American "military trusteeship" seems firmly in place.

Latin America Today   Throughout Latin America, a certain amount of polarization has taken place since the Alliance for Progress days of the early 1960s. Of the 275 million Latin Americans, about half live under right-wing military governments, less than one in ten under Marxist-Socialism, and the rest under governments that wobble uncertainly in between. The landowners, big business, the church hierarchy, and in most cases the army, stand on one side; the growing mass of the underprivileged rank on the other. In Brazil, for example, 3 percent of the nation's 90 million people own 62 percent of the land. Eighty-two percent of South American industry is owned by U.S. capitalism, and yet these North American investors, however resented, employ 2 million South Americans, pay one fifth of the taxes, and produce one third of the exports. Without them, the economy would collapse.

The shaky democracies of the early 1960s were simply not up to the massive job of effecting the needed change in the continent's life. A Communist surge from the bottom would probably fare no better. In June of 1970, Argentina's president, former General Juan Carlos Ongania, was removed from office by a military junta. Most citizens ignored the affair, saying, "This is a military matter. What have politics to do with me?" This is a common attitude in the area and suggests a solution that may be more likely than communism to prevail in Latin America. The military strong man has long been a familiar figure. The tradition goes back to Símon Bolívar and José de San Martin, who drove Spain out of the land. Most South American military regimes are convinced, with reason, that the civilian politicians are corruptible and incompetent, and there are many examples where military groups have made acceptable improvements. One of these was the predominantly neo-fascist government of Argentina when Perón and his Peronistas took political power from the aristocracy. They put power not only into their own hands, but into those of the middle and working classes as well.

Other military cliques have been composed of dedicated young officers. Such was the group that came to power in 1968 in Peru under General Juan Velasco Alvarado. With the intent of strengthening the position of the state in order to bring changes for the better, many large foreign holdings in the country have been expropriated. Some middle-class and upper-class people have been forced to leave. But if anything is to be done to rectify the swelling poverty of the masses, there may be no better course at present than this new military socialism.

In Bolivia, General Juan José Torres followed a similar path until his overthrow in August, 1971. In

Brazil, the Escola Superior de Guerra, modeled after Washington's War College, has not only concerned itself with matters of war, revolution, and prevention of foreign subversion, but has undertaken the study of economics and sociology. The old image of the bandoliered, bemedaled autocrat has shifted to that of technical expert, very much concerned with the national future. In effect, it is a Latin American form of Nasserism.

The extreme alternative on the Left, advocated less loudly now by Cuba's Castro, has been called Jacobin after a group in the French Revolution that would never compromise. Lenin used the term for those Communists who insisted irrevocably on the bloody revolution of the proletariat. Such is the implacable doctrine of the New Left in Latin America, which has turned its back on Soviet gradualism. The jungles are handy for prolonged guerrilla tactics, and the old-line political Communists are "establishment" and obsolete as far as these radicals are concerned. Characteristic are Uruguay's Tupamaros, a terrorist organization. It refuses, or is perhaps intellectually unable, to define its political and revolutionary goals beyond bringing down the present system through bombings, burnings, and murder. Such an approach provides no long-term solution. Though Nasserism may seem a sad substitute for democracy, it is at least preferable to revolution for revolution's sake. From an objective point of view, it is about the best present alternative for the social crisis that confronts Latin America.

Conclusion: The Emerging Future

When the sweet old lady who always had a kind word for everyone was asked to comment on Satan, she remarked, after a moment's hesitation, "Well, I certainly think he's hard-working." The phrase can suitably head up a list of communism's strengths and virtues. In the material world, progress has been staggering. From preponderant illiteracy after World War I, Russia has moved to over 67 percent literacy. There are, per capita, more doctors and engineers there than in the United States. Like Satan, communism measures its success in very materialistic terms, and herein lies their mutual sin against the human spirit. Both are powerful adversaries in the material world, but they will founder at the strength of a social order in which the ends of morality, individual free expression, and justice are served.

Thus far, communism has had its major successes in nations where the governments have been torn by war and where the mass of the population has been existing at near survival levels. Only where misery is rampant will a country surrender its measure of stability for the bloody hazard of revolution. This incendiary discontent, according to Marxian doctrine, was expected from the working class of factory laborers, but much has changed in the West since those early capitalistic days. Though Marx imagined the lot of these workers getting worse and worse as capitalistic profits were extracted at the expense of their wages, such projected inequities have been balanced out by the progressive income tax and the minimum wage.

Other factors Marx misjudged were the adaptability of the capitalist class and the growing power of trade unions. Theodore Roosevelt initiated the Square Deal; Woodrow Wilson, the New Freedom; Franklin D. Roosevelt, the New Deal. All moved to give labor a stake in the system. Communism may label such measures, as they did the rise of the British Labour party, clever plots on the part of big business to keep itself in power, but the fact remains that the exploited proletariat of the nineteenth century no longer exists. And even if the bulk of labor calls itself the Communist party, as in France, that does not make it a revolutionary force. The object is simply a strong voting voice to enhance their own material interests in the system as it exists.

The curious irony of present-day communism is, on the one hand, its failure to arouse the prospering workers of the world to revolution despite sharp increases in industrial expansion. On the other hand, communization of agriculture has been a uniform disappointment, and yet it is in agrarian countries that the Communist appeal still has revolutionary strength.

Industrial success has come very largely at the price of doctrine. In the early days of the Soviet Union, wage levels reflected the idea that all workers were comrades toiling together, and the spread of income from the lowest manual worker to the highest plant manager was no more than one to two. Now, with the grudging admission that men work for personal, not utopian goals, wages of some have been raised to the point where the spread is fifteen to one. That isn't the only shift from theory toward capitalist reality. Planners have moved from the old command economy of the

Stalinist era to the Western notion of an economy responsive to demand. The goal of gross production that made for shoddy goods and hoarding of material to meet quotas has given way to more autonomy of management at the factory level.

Individual enterprise has by no means vanished in many Communist countries. The best planning system leaves unavoidable gaps, and there is always someone to make pitchforks or, should the demand exist, sell tropical fish. Farmers cling tenaciously to their land, and, where the opportunity avails, will farm independently at the expense of the cooperative or collective. An extreme example of possessiveness occurred in Russia, where a farmer so cherished his small apple orchard that, to thwart marauding boys, he planted land mines. This sense of ownership and of belonging is hard to train away. Many psychologists would argue it is basic to human nature, and, though the farmer in question stepped on one of his own mines and lost an eye for his trouble, a spirit like his is apt to cause orthodox Communists more, not less, trouble in years to come.

If this individualism is a threat to orthodox communism, its converse, bureaucratic conformity, is even more of a menace to the neocommunism of the future. Kosygin and Brezhnev wear gray flannel suits. Their revolutionary forefathers were great social innovators, but they represent an entrenched political orthodoxy that resists experimentation. Ideas from outside the Soviet Union are suspect. Any individualism or criticism, however constructive in intent, is frowned upon. Khrushchev looked at modern art and commented with disgust that it had been "painted with a donkey's tail." The new regime has intensified the attack on arts and letters. Such closed totalitarianism cannot progress in a world where change is the only certainty.

A more obvious and constant stumbling block to the realization of Communist goals has been religion. As an atheist, Marx regarded religion simply as the "spiritual aroma" of a dying system; it was not worth a major attack. His followers have taken it more seriously as antirevolutionary, "the pus of a sick world," and one of the causes for the failures of the proletarian revolution. Communist doctrine predicted that science would eventually answer all questions and that a Communist paradise would replace a spiritual one. Superficially, communism has mimicked religion, particularly Catholicism. It is possible to point to similarities between the structure of the Vatican and the Kremlin. Original sin becomes private property; Marx, Lenin, and Stalin become Father, Son, and Holy Ghost; paradise, the communist millennium. Whatever the similarities, religion answers one compelling question that communism never can: the question of human mortality. Without death, there would be little, if any, religion, but as long as that unattractive mystery persists, religion will have a following in the world at large as well as within the Communist sanctuaries.

Soviet policy has generally been to contain rather than eradicate religion. Many theological colleges have been closed and priests' licenses suspended, yet those churches that remain open are packed on Sundays. Clergymen, such as the recently released Cardinal Mindszenty of Hungary, have been jailed and persecuted for stepping outside the church into politics. In the long run, the contest is apt to remain a standoff. In such firmly religious countries as Poland, communism and religion have learned to get along together. There is no reason why practical communism with its ideologies softened cannot function in cooperation with Islam or the Christian Church.

While Soviet communism and the Christian Church, though in conflict, show structural similarities, the mystique of Chinese communism can, in part, be explained from absorption of oriental religious traditions. Principally, these are Taoism, which stresses the meditative way to inner tranquillity and enlightenment, and Confucianism, which exhorts that all intellectual and moral energy be channeled for self-perfection, the common good, and social and universal peace. Here is no clash of monolithic institutions such as exists between the Russian party and the Catholic Church, but an adaptable, philosophic mold into which Maoism fits with ease.

In the former colonial areas of the world, communism has had to face another grave disappointment. Russia has always represented herself as the spearhead of the drive to overcome imperialism and colonialism. Now Western colonialism in its most conspicuous areas, Africa and Asia, had all but vanished, not, as the Communists hoped, by revolution, but by voluntary surrender. These new nations have their problems, social and political. Communism is only one of the solutions being applied, and not the most popular one at that. Meanwhile, Russia remains in the position of being the greatest colonial power on earth. While Britain and France were painfully severing their colonial relations, Russia was securing hers in Georgia and Turkestan.

Turkestan is Russia's largest colony in Asia. Traditionally, it was a Muslim region, with its own identity, but under Soviet dominion it was divided up into national soviet republics and consequently vanished as an entity from Russian maps. Political leaders who resisted this absorption went to prison or before the firing squad. The Turkestan poet Cholpan wrote a poem to the Russian Communists: "Pack your suitcases, make Turkestan free." He, too, was shot. This duplicity, as well as Red China's absorption of Tibet, has not been lost on the nonaligned nations. They are also aware of Russia's actions in Hungary and Czechoslovakia. It is less likely that the future of world communism will be decided in Moscow, Peking, or Washington, D.C., than in such uncommitted capitals as Delhi, Rio de Janeiro, and Dar es Salaam.

Western democracies can give no single answer to communism. In a free society with an intellectual heritage of many philosophies, there must be many answers. Apart from any philosophy, there is one psychological fact ignored by communism in its obsession with economics, and that factor is a sense of belonging. This feeling is manifest in international terms as nationalism; and it ranges from the extremes of Gaullism down to the self-importance of the smallest emergent nation. Mother tongues and national cultures will prevail over communist philosophy even as they have prevailed when put to the test in Russia and Red China.

Nationalism more than anything else has broken up the monolithic front that communism once presented to the world. The old objective of world revolution can now, at best, be envisioned as individual national revolutions, and the Communist leaders of today cannot question that the old dream of a united struggle to the death against capitalism is a desperate one that would cost them far more than they are willing to pay.

There is a refreshing irony in this grudging realization, East and West, that both communism and democratic capitalism are apt to be around for a long time. It has developed into a limited adversary relationship between the Soviet Union and the United States. Formerly, communism waited on the thought that capitalism would vanish through pure economic logic. The United States hoped for a democratic counterrevolution in Russia. Both have proved false hopes. Though the ultimate political expectations of these two countries may remain irreconcilable, this fact has tended to recede into the hazy future. Between the two countries have developed parallel, if not mutual, interests. Both have concern for growing nationalism in other parts of the world. Both are aware of the undesirability of the spread of nuclear weapons. The developing situation might even be called an alliance between the two world powers against war between themselves. It does not mean an end to friction, but it does imply restraint: the United States in Hungary and in Cuba; Russia in Vietnam and in the Cuban missile crisis. The provocations are there if either country wants to use them. A prime example was the played-down opposition of American fighter pilots versus Soviet-operated missile bases in North Vietnam.

The goal of Communist world revolution is further away now than it was thirty years ago. Marxian doctrines have to a large extent been abandoned, but even if they never fitted the world situation, this philosophy must be given credit for inspiring the most major social change since the middle of the nineteenth century. Its impact endures even though its theories have not been specifically carried out. The philosophical goal of communism has always been admirable, but it seems no more attainable now than when it was conceived. For such a material paradise, incredible abundance is vital. No Communist country has come close to such requisite prosperity, though most have made very real progress from poverty to industrialization. For such a paradise, people must be inspired by different motives than are known in the West. They must have leaders of complete dedication and selflessness. Neither Russia nor China has molded such supermen, and they are not likely to in the foreseeable future. However, they have galvanized their nations into productive efforts formerly unimagined.

A true Communist society requires absolute equality among its members. Such equality is not part of the human condition and not part of existing Communist societies, where power seems just as sweet as it does anywhere else in the world. In an ideal Communist society, the people must be free, but this has been realized less than any other ideal by Communist governments. They remain, by and large, totalitarian and intolerant of individual expression or criticism.

Communism as it is practiced today can never lead to the Marxist millennium. In many ways it demands that people live contrary to their instincts. Like Cromwell's Puritans, will it simply fade away because man reaches a point where he prefers comfort and entertainment to stern moral purpose? Probably not; but to survive, it must adjust to a changing world. It is to be hoped that with increasing stability, its totalitarian and embattled aspects will be laid aside.

Definitions

Anarchism The political belief that all oppression comes from the state, which must be overthrown. Communists have always opposed the theory of anarchism.

Bolshevik Means in Russian, literally, "the majority." The word was first used by the Communists in 1903 when Lenin caused a split in the Russian Social Democratic Labor party over whether revolution should be achieved by democratic evolution or by violence. Lenin favored the latter course and won the support of the majority of the party for the seizure of power during the revolution. The term has become a synonym for "Communist." *See also* Menshevik.

Bourgeoisie In Communist terms, the social class that owns the means of production and can live on its resources without having to sell its labor to survive. Originally the French word had meant simply those who lived in towns.

Cadre The Communist party members who serve as a nucleus in their offices or institutions and are capable of training others in party functions. The Chinese party relies heavily on carefully indoctrinated cadres.

Centrism The doctrine that held that the revolution in Russia had to pass through a bourgeois stage before socialism could be developed. Trotsky supported this idea, but Lenin denounced it.

Class struggle The conflict among economic groups in

society that Marx believed was the cause of all social and historical change.

Classless society The unified social and economic existence that, in communist thinking, is the final stage in history and thus the goal of communism. *See also* Millennium.

Collectivization The process of bringing land under the control of large state-owned and state-operated farms.

Cominform The Communist Information Bureau. Organized in 1947 for the purpose of bringing the Eastern European satellite countries and the Communist parties of France and Italy under the control of one semipolitical body and to aid in the spread of communism throughout the world. The Cominform was dissolved in 1956, three years after the death of Stalin.

Comintern The first truly international Communist convention, formally called the Third International. Organized in 1919, it guided the spread of international communism until the organization was dissolved in 1943. *See also* Internationals.

Commune A large state-run, involuntary unit into which Chinese peasants were organized during the Great Leap Forward of the late 1950s.

Cult of personality, or cult of the individual The aberration from Marxist doctrine that occurs when a leader sets himself as an individual above communist principles. In 1956 Khrushchev denounced Stalin's rule for its cult of personality.

Democratic centralism A term used by Lenin to indicate a combination of dictatorship with his idea of democracy, which actually meant merely mass participation in political activities.

Dialectical materialism A theory that explains the course of history in terms of the economic struggle that takes place between classes in society. The theory was developed by Marx and Engels, who based their thinking on the ideas of Hegel.

Exploitation A term used by Marx for the practice of taking from the worker labor of more value than is recompensed by his wages.

First International *See* Internationals.

Five-year plan Beginning in 1927, the Soviet Union established a series of economic plans that set objectives for industry and agriculture to be realized within the five-year scope of the plan.

Imperialism In communist phraseology, the last stage of capitalism, in which free competition is replaced by monopoly.

Industrial Workers of the World (IWW) A labor group formed in 1905, nicknamed the Wobblies. The organization's position was anti-war and tended toward communism.

Internationals The First International or the International Workingmen's Association was established in London by Marx and Engels in 1864 to link national workers' societies and further Marxian aims. The organization dissolved in 1876. The Second International, formed in 1889, was made up of Socialist parties. For the Third International, *see* Comintern.

Jacobin In Marxist vocabulary the extremist group who insist on the rule of the revolutionary proletariat all the way to the dawn of communism. The term originally meant the extremist political group active in the French Revolution.

Kulak In Russia Communist terms, a prosperous peasant farmer who profited from the oppression of other farmers and resisted collectivization. In the 1930s large numbers of kulaks were liquidated.

Leap In the Marxist theory of history a "leap" is a break with gradual evolution, causing an abrupt emergence or a new reality.

Maoism Marxism as developed in China by Mao Tsetung, placing emphasis on revolutionary peasantry rather than upon industrial workers.

Menshevik Means in Russian, literally, "the minority." The word was first used by the Communists in 1903 in the split in the Russian Social Democratic Labor party over whether revolution should be achieved by democratic evolution or by violence. The Mensheviks believed in the evolutionary process. *See also* Bolshevik.

Millennium In Marxist phraseology, the ultimate classless society marked by a maximum of human goodness and cooperation maintained without the control of governmental apparatus. *See also* Classless society.

Party line   The positions taken and tactics endorsed by the world Communist movement.

Politburo   The policy-making and executive committee of a national Communist party.

Pravda   Literally, "the truth." The official Soviet Russian newspaper.

Presidium   The permanent committee that exercises executive power in a Communist country. The Soviet presidium is selected from the Supreme Soviet.

Proletariat   Wage earners, in particular; industrial workers.

Revisionism   In communist terminology, the attempt to change the approach of communism from a revolutionary movement to one working by evolutionary means to achieve socialism.

Soviet   In Russian, literally, "a council." Under communism the soviet became the fundamental unit of government. Revolutionary councils, or soviets, were first created in 1905 and were made up of factory workers. The government in Russia today rests upon a hierarchy of soviets. *See also* Supreme Soviet.

Supreme Soviet   The highest body of governmental power in Soviet Russia, which elects the supreme court, the procurator-general, and the presidium. *See also* Presidium.

Surplus value   The communist term for a capitalist's profits. According to Marx, the difference between the actual value of a worker's labor, as determined by the market price of the product, and the amount the worker is paid in wages represents the surplus value, which the worker is denied and the capitalist takes as profit.

Trotskyism   Specifically, the views of Trotsky, and generally, any deviation from the party line.

Vanguard   The elite, the Communists, who lead the way to revolution.

Yezhovshchina   The great Soviet purges of the late 1930s.

Biographies

Allende Gossens, Dr. Salvador (1908–1973): The son of a provincial Chilean lawyer, Allende studied medicine at the University of Chile. Helped found the Chilean Socialist party. He was first elected a national deputy in 1937 and became the first Marxist president in 1970. Deposed in 1973 and died in the upheaval an apparent suicide.

Brezhnev, Leonid (1906–   ): Born in the Ukraine, he received a technical education and held various local engineering positions and political offices. From 1941 to 1946 Brezhnev was a political officer in the Soviet Army and subsequently began moving up through party ranks. Since 1966 he has been General Secretary of the CPSU.

Castro, Fidel (1927–   ): Educated at Jesuit schools in Santiago and Havana, Cuba, and at Havana University, Castro began a law practice in Havana and became active in the political opposition to the Batista regime. On July 26, 1953, he began an insurrection, which failed. After a brief exile in Mexico, he returned to Cuba with an armed force and drove Batista out. He has been prime minister of Cuba since 1959.

Chou En-lai (1898?–1976): Born in Szechwan Province, of a Mandarin family, Chou studied in Paris and in Germany. He helped to found the Chinese Communist party and the Chinese Red Army, and he took part in the Long March. Chou had been a member of the central committee of the party since 1926, and from 1949 he was premier of China.

Engels, Friedrich (1820–1895): Born in Barmen, Germany, the son of a textile manufacturer, he met Karl Marx in 1844. Three years later they wrote the *Communist Manifesto*, and then founded the First International Workingmen's Association. Engels' last years were devoted to editing the second and third volumes of Marx's *Capital*, as well as writing several books of his own.

Guevara, Dr. Ernesto (Che) (1928–1967): A native of Rosario, Argentina, he was educated as a physician. He was active in the opposition to the dictatorship of Perón in Argentina. Subsequently Guevara lived as a revolutionary in several South American countries and in Mexico, where he met and joined the exiled Cuban forces of Castro. After fighting successfully in the Cuban Revolution, Guevara was active in Cuban government affairs until 1965, when he left the island to return to guerrilla activities in South America. He was captured and executed by Bolivian government troops in 1967.

Hegel, Georg Wilhelm Friedrich (1770–1831): German idealist philosopher who influenced Marx and Engels, particularly with his theory that history was a process of thesis and antithesis making for struggle which results in synthesis.

Ho Chi Minh (1890?–1969): His name means literally "he who shines"; his real name is uncertain. Born in Annam (now a part of Vietnam), the son of a minor government official, at about nineteen Ho joined the crew of a French merchant ship, traveled the world for several years, and settled in Paris during World War I. He joined the Communist party and went to Moscow for political training. He was sent to China in 1925 and began his work of organizing a Communist underground of Vietnamese exiles. From 1946 he fought against the French in Vietnam until he was victorious, in 1954, and became president of the Democratic Republic of [North] Vietnam.

Kerenski, Alexander (1881–1970): Russian jurist, born in Simbirsk and educated at Tashkent and Saint Petersburg University. He was briefly premier of the provisional government that existed in Russia after the February Revolution in 1917. After the Bolshevik victory in November, 1917, Kerenski fled Russia, stayed in several countries, and after 1940 lived in the United States until his death.

Khrushchev, Nikita Sergeevich (1894–1971): He was born in the village of Kalinovka in the Ukraine, worked on his father's farm, became a shepherd, miner, and locksmith. Khrushchev joined the Communist party in 1918, and not until 1920 did he receive his first formal education at a Communist party school in the factory where he worked. He rose persistently in Stalin's bureaucracy and prevailed in the power struggle in 1957 after Stalin's death. He was premier of the USSR until 1964, when he was ousted for his too liberal views and policy failures. He was allowed to live peacefully in retirement until his death in 1971.

Kosygin, Aleksei (1904–   ): Born in Saint Petersburg (now Leningrad), he received a technical education in textile manufacturing and became a shop superintendent in a Leningrad factory. His first important political post was that of manager of the industrial and transport department of the CPSU. Kosygin rose through a number of party and government offices. During World War II he was vice chairman of the Council of People's Commissars. He had been chairman of the USSR council of ministers since 1964.

Krupskaya, Nadezhda Konstantinovna (1868–1939): Lenin's wife. They met at a pancake festival in 1894. When Lenin was sent to Siberia for his Communist activities she carried on his "League of Struggle" until she too was sent to Siberia, where they were married. Until Lenin's death in 1924 they worked closely together.

Lenin, Nicolai (Vladimir Ilich Ulyanov) (1870–1924): The leader of the Russian Revolution, he was born in Simbirsk into a middle-class family. In 1891 he became a lawyer and in 1897 was exiled to Siberia for revolutionary activities. After his term ended he went to Europe and became the leader of the Bolshevik party. In 1917 he persuaded the German government to help him return to Russia and there he took over

Marxist leadership. He ran the Soviet state until his death in 1924 and played a major role in the theoretical development of communism.

Mao Tse-tung (1893-   ): Mao was born into a peasant family in Hunan Province and educated as a teacher. He was a founding member of the Communist party of China in 1921 and active in education, youth organizations, and peasant unions. He led the Long March to escape the forces of Chiang Kai-shek and subsequently became the chairman of the Communist party of China.

Marx, Karl (1818–1883): The father of international communism, Marx was born in Germany. He studied law at the Bonn, Berlin, and Jena universities, and in 1843 was banished from Germany for his radical views. Banished from France, and then from Belgium, he fled to London in 1849. The year before, in Brussels, he published his *Communist Manifesto*. In the British Museum he worked on *Capital*. The First International Workingmen's Association was organized by Marx and Engels in 1864. Until the end of his life he worked on *Capital*, only the first volume of which was published while he lived.

Plekhanov, Georgi (1857–1918): Second only to Lenin as Russian Marxist, he was instrumental in forming the first Russian Marxist party. He joined Lenin in editing the newspaper *Iskra*. The two split in 1903 with Plekhanov leading the Menshevik faction. He took no part in Russian revolution.

Stalin, Joseph (Iosif Vissarionovich Dzhugashvili) (1879–1953): Born the son of a shoemaker, Stalin was expelled from school for radicalism. By 1912 he was the editor of *Pravda*. His role in the revolution was minor but later as general secretary of the central committee he gained control of the party, defeating Trotsky in a struggle for power following Lenin's death. Thereafter Stalin ruled supreme in the USSR until his death in 1953.

Tito, Marshal (Josip Broz) (1892–   ): He was born in Zagorje, Croatia. He trained as a mechanic and served in the Austro-Hungarian Army in the First World War and was imprisoned in Russian concentration camps. He took part in the Russian Revolution. Returned to Yugoslavia, he became active in trade union organization and in the Yugoslav Communist party. Tito fought in the Spanish Civil War, organized Yugoslav partisan resistance forces against the German occupation of Yugoslavia, and served as president of the National Liberation Committee. From 1945 to 1953 Tito was prime minister and since 1953 he has been president of the Republic of Yugoslavia.

Trotsky, Leon (Lev Davydovich Bronstein) (1877–1940): Born near Elisavetgrad, educated in Odessa, in 1898 Trotsky was banished to Siberia for revolutionary activities but escaped to London and joined Lenin. In 1903, however, he joined the Menshevik faction and did not rejoin Lenin politically until 1917. With Lenin in hiding after July, 1917, Trotsky was in command of Bolshevik maneuvers that led to the October takeover of the Russian government. Later he created the Red Army while Stalin was gaining control of the party machinery. Their power struggle culminated in 1927 with Trotsky being expelled from the party and banished from the Soviet Union two years later. In 1940, while in exile in Mexico, he was murdered by Stalin's agents.

Bibliography of Sources

Aczel, Tamas, ed. *Ten Years After: The Hungarian Revolution in the Perspective of History*. New York: Holt Rinehart and Winston, 1966.

Aguilar, Luis E. *Marxism in Latin America*. New York: Alfred Knopf, 1968.

Blanchard, Paul. *Communism, Democracy, and Catholic Power*. Boston: Beacon Press, 1951.

Campbell, John C. *Tito's Separate Road*. New York: Harper and Row, 1967.

Chai, Ch'u and Chai, Winberg. *The Changing Society of China*. N.Y., Toronto, London: The New American Library, 1969.

Coughlan, Robert. *Tropical Africa*. Life World Library, New York: Time Inc., 1962.

Crow, John A. *Mexico Today*. New York: Harper and Brothers, 1957.

De Koster, Lester. *Vocabulary of Communism*. Grand Rapids, Mich.: William Eerdmans Publishing Co., 1964.

Dellin, L. A. D., ed. *Bulgaria*. New York: Praeger, 1957.

Deutsch, André. *Communist Economy Under Change*. London: The Institute of Economic Affairs, Rowan Press, 1963.

Dornberg, John. *The Other Germany*. Garden City, New York: Doubleday, 1968.

Draper, Theodore. *American Communism and Soviet Russia*. New York: The Viking Press, 1960.

Ebenstein, William. *Today's Isms*. Englewood Cliffs, N.J.: Prentice-Hall, 1954.

Eliot, Alexander. *Greece*. Life World Library, New York: Time Inc., 1963.

Fast, Howard. *The Naked God: The Writer and the Communist Party*. New York: Praeger, 1957.

Fessler, Loren. *China*. Life World Library, New York: Time Inc., 1963.

Floyd, David. *Rumania: Russia's Dissident Ally*. New York: Praeger, 1965.

Fremantle, Anne, ed. *Communism: Basic Writings*. New York, Toronto, London: New American Library, 1970.

Gretton, George, ed. *Communism and Colonialism*. New York: St. Martin's Press, 1964.

Harrison, J. F. C. *Quest for the New Moral World*. New York: Charles Scribner's Sons, 1969.

Hendel, Samuel, ed. *The Soviet Crucible*. Princeton, N.J.: D. Van Nostrand Co., 1959.

Herreshoff, David. *American Disciples of Marx*. Detroit: Wayne State University Press, 1967.

Hoffman, George, and Neal, Fred Warner. *Yugoslavia and the New Communism*. New York: Twentieth Century Fund, 1962.

Hoover, J. Edgar. *On Communism*. New York: Random House, 1969.

Houn, Franklin, W. *A Short History of Chinese Communism*. Englewood Cliffs, N.J.: Prentice-Hall, 1967.

Huberman, Leo, and Sweezy, Paul M. *Socialism in Cuba*. New York and London: Monthly Review Press, 1969.

Karnow, Stanley. *Southeast Asia*. Life World Library. New York: Time Inc., 1967.

Ketchum, Richard M., and Brunberg, Abraham, eds. *What Is Communism*. New York: E. P. Dutton, 1963.

Khadduri, Majid. *Independent Iraq*. London, New York, Karachi: Oxford University Press, 1960.

Kirkpatrick, Jeane J., ed. *The Strategy of Deception*. New York: Farrar, Straus, and Giroux, 1963.

Kurzman, Dan. *Subversion of the Innocents*. New York: Random House, 1963.

Latham, Earl. *The Communist Controversy in Washing-*

ton. Cambridge, Mass.: Harvard University Press, 1966.

Lawrence, John. *A History of Russia,* second revised edition. New York: New American Library, 1969.

Lewis, John Wilson. *Major Doctrines of Communist China.* New York: W. W. Norton, 1964.

Lichtheim, George. *A Short History of Socialism.* New York, Washington: Praeger, 1970.

Lobkowicz, Nicholas, ed. *Marx and the Western World.* Notre Dame, London: University of Notre Dame Press, 1967.

MacIntyre, Alasdair. *Marxism and Christianity.* New York: Schocken Books, 1968.

Mannheim, Karl. *Ideology and Utopia.* New York: Harcourt, Brace and World. A Harvest Book, 1936.

Manuel, Frank E., and Manuel, Fritzie P. *French Utopias.* New York: The Free Press, 1966.

Mead, Margaret. *Cooperation and Competition Among Primitive Peoples.* New York, London: McGraw-Hill, 1937.

Payne, Robert. *The Civil War in Spain.* Greenwich, Conn.: Fawcett Publications Inc., 1962.

Peterson, William, ed. *The Realities of World Communism.* Englewood Cliffs, N.J.: Prentice-Hall, 1963.

Russell, Bertrand. *The Practice and Theory of Bolshevism.* New York: Simon and Schuster, 1964.

Savage, Katherine. *The Story of Marxism and Communism.* New York: New American Library, 1969.

Scalapino, Robert A., ed. *The Communist Revolution in Asia.* Englewood Cliffs, N.J.: Prentice-Hall, 1965.

Schatten, Fritz. *Communism in Africa.* New York: Praeger, 1966.

Schmitt, Karl M. *Communism in Mexico.* Austin: University of Texas Press, 1965.

Staar, Richard F. *Poland 1944–1962.* Louisiana State University Press, 1962.

Stewart, Desmond. *The Arab World.* Life World Library. New York: Time Inc., 1968.

Stillman, Edmund. *The Balkans.* Life World Library, New York: Time Inc., 1964.

Swearingen, Rodger, ed. *Soviet and Chinese Communist Power in the World Today.* New York, London: Basic Books, 1966.

Swift, Lindsay. *Brook Farm.* New York: Corinth Books, 1961.

Watson, Hugh Seton. *From Lenin to Khrushchev.* New York, London: Praeger, 1960.

Wilson, William E. *The Angel and the Serpent, the Story of New Harmony.* Bloomington, Ind.: Indiana University Press, 1964.

Index

MILTON MELTZER
brilliantly evokes the shocking and glorious moments of our history

☐ **SLAVERY:**
   From the Rise of Western Civilization to Today
A two-volume survey of slavery, combined into one, from ancient times through modern. "An excellent overview." —Best Books of the Year Selection, *School Library Journal*. $1.75 (98019-4)

☐ **UNDERGROUND MAN**
Josh lived in a state of fear: he knew he could be sent to prison, or even hanged, for helping a black escape from a slave state. But Josh had found his calling as an abolitionist on the Ohio River and he knew he would return. "A realistic story, based on actual events and drawn from contemporary sources."—*The Booklist*. 95¢ (98627-3)

☐ **HUNTED LIKE A WOLF**
"A well-known writer of American biography and history here considers the seven-year Seminole War in detail. Beginning with Columbus' attitude toward the Indians and quoting many writers' descriptions of them, Meltzer emphasizes that fraud, corruption, trickery, and violence were and are even today the white man's weapons against the Indian." —*The Booklist*. "Dramatic self-contained case study."—*The Kirkus Review*. 95¢ (93788-4)

Laurel-Leaf Editions

At your local bookstore or use this handy coupon for ordering:

Dell | **DELL BOOKS**
P.O. BOX 1000, PINEBROOK, N.J. 07058

Please send me the books I have checked above. I am enclosing $ _____ (please add 75¢ per copy to cover postage and handling). Send check or money order—no cash or C.O.D.'s. Please allow up to 8 weeks for shipment.

Mr/Mrs/Miss _____

Address _____

City _____ State/Zip _____

"Unique in its uncompromising portrait of human cruelty and conformity."
—*School Library Journal*

THE CHOCOLATE WAR

by Robert Cormier

A compelling combination of
Lord Of The Flies **and** ***A Separate Peace***

Jerry Renault, a New England high school student, is stunned by his mother's recent death and appalled by the way his father sleepwalks through life. At school, he resists the leader of a secret society by refusing to sell candies for the chocolate sale, wondering: Do I dare disturb the universe?

"Masterfully structured and rich in theme. . . . The action is well crafted, well timed, suspenseful; complex ideas develop and unfold with clarity."
—*The New York Times*

"Readers will respect the uncompromising ending."
—*Kirkus Reviews*

"Close enough to the reality of the tribal world of adolescence to make one squirm."—*Best Sellers*

Laurel-Leaf Fiction $1.50

At your local bookstore or use this handy coupon for ordering:

Dell

DELL BOOKS
The Chocolate War $1.50 **(94459-7)**
P.O. BOX 1000, PINEBROOK, N.J. 07058

Please send me the above title. I am enclosing $_____
(please add 75¢ per copy to cover postage and handling). Send check or money order—no cash or C.O.D.'s. Please allow up to 8 weeks for shipment.

Mr/Mrs/Miss_____

Address_____

City_____ State/Zip_____